Courtesy NRHA Reiner

A LOFT ENTERPRISES BOOK

REINMAKER
The Dale Wilkinson Story

By Frank Holmes

REINMAKER

Published by

LOFT
Enterprises, LLC
2767 Jeep Road
Abilene, KS 67410

Cover Design
Sandy Cochran
Fort Collins, Colorado

Cover Photos
Dale Wilkinson 1994 *photo courtesy* NRHA Reiner
Dale Wilkinson Cutting *photo courtesy the Wilkinson Family*
Dale Wilkinson Reining *photo courtesy the Wilkinson Family*

Design, Typography, and Production
Sandy Cochran Graphic Design
Fort Collins, Colorado

Copy Editors
Carol Plybon
Abilene, Kansas

Dan Streeter
Hurst, Texas

Printing
Central Plains Book Manufacturing Company
Winfield, Kansas

©2013 by LOFT Enterprises, LLC
All rights reserved

Copyright Notice: *This book is copyrighted by* LOFT Enterprises,LLC *and therefore protected by federal copyright law. No material may be copied, FAXed, electronically transmitted, or otherwise used without express written permission.*
Requests must be submitted in writing.

First Printing: April 2013

Hardcover

ISBN 978-1-62620-452-2

Dedication

This book is dedicated to
Lucinda Mary Wilkinson
Loving wife, nurturing mother, steadfast friend,
The backbone of a successful horse business with her life partner Dale.

This book is also dedicated to the millions of students and fans
of cutting and reining horses all over the world.
May you ride and train like Dale Wilkinson.

INTRODUCTION

I knew Dale Wilkinson for a long time, more than 40 years, and I've never met anybody like him. It took a while to get to know him well enough to understand him. He had a personality that disarmed everybody. He was down to earth, with a wonderful sense of humor. You would like him immediately. And, what Dale said, you could always count on. He was stubborn, but a man of his word.

I became his vet soon after I arrived in Findlay, Ohio, and set up a veterinary practice. Dale always kept me on my toes. He never let me know if I was good or bad. It took a while to earn his respect.

When the phone would ring, and I'd be called to Dale's farm, it was never a chore to go. Circumstances could be medically challenging, but being in the atmosphere of his presence – and the farm, the horses and the people that I met there – was always enjoyable.

I remember Mr Gun Smoke, probably the most athletic horse I've ever been around, and with a personality and disposition equally as great. And, you could tell there was a unique bond between Dale and that horse. It didn't take long to realize that Dale had a very special talent in his ability to communicate his feelings to that horse and that horse to him.

His farm was a busy place at breeding season with all the people who came there to have their mares bred to Mr Gun Smoke. The progeny he produced are still remembered and are still out there today. That horse sure made a difference in Dale's life.

Dale was a wonderful teacher who conveyed his talent to others in a very unique way. He didn't tell them the answers. He would give them suggestions, and let them figure it out for themselves. Every year, around time for Congress, horsemen would come to see Dale for advice on how their horses could do better.

There are many people who have drifted through Findlay, Ohio, and become world-famous because he was their teacher. Nobody worked any harder than Dale. He was probably the most passionate horse trainer who ever lived. I don't think that he ever went to sleep at night that he wasn't still thinking about riding and training.

Because of Dale, The University of Findlay has the finest instructional staff in equestrian studies in the country. I can say that without reservations or hesitation. There have been so many successful people in the horse industry because of Dale, and that's why this book had to be written.

C. Richard Beckett, D.V.M.

C. Richard Beckett

Acknowledgments

Any book of this depth requires the contribution of numerous individuals. Because we lost Frank Holmes before he could complete the extensive list of those he wished to thank, many who did contribute will go nameless, but you know who you are.

I do know that Frank would first and foremost send special thanks to the Wilkinson family for their interviews, e-mails, photos and input, but especially for their patience and understanding.

He would also thank the University of Findlay who funded this book and showed extreme patience and empathy as Frank's final illness caused delay after delay in its completion.

To these worthy individuals, I would like to add a special acknowledgement to Loyce Holmes, Frank's widow, without whose support this book could not have been published. I want to send a special thank you to Sandy Cochran of Fort Collins, Colorado, who was the book's sole designer and graphic artist.

And to all those who will read and treasure this and all other books written by Frank, thank you.

Carol J. Plybon

LOFT Partner and Business Manager

Table of Contents

Page

- 6   Introduction—By C. Richard Beckett, D.V.M.
- 10   Prologue—The Buck Stops Here
- 12   Chapter 1—A Son of the Soil
- 18   Chapter 2—Partnering Up
- 24   Chapter 3—In From the Range
- 34   Chapter 4—Millstream Stables
- 46   Chapter 5—A Pair of Kings
- 56   Chapter 6—An Industry is Born
- 62   Chapter 7—Millstream South
- 70   Chapter 8—Where There's Smoke
- 81   Chapter 9—A Smokin' Sire
- 86   Chapter 10   Higher Education
- 94   Chapter 11—Southern Comfort
- 98   Chapter 12   The Legend and the Legacy
- 108   Epilogue—You Can Let Go
- 110   Photo Index
- 114   Author's Profile

PROLOGUE

Findlay, Ohio, mid-summer or early fall, 1942—much of the world is locked in the life-and-death, "good-against-evil" struggle that is World War II. Responding to the aggression of the Axis powers Nazi Germany, Italy and Japan, the United States is embroiled in the conflict in both the European and Pacific theaters of war.

On the home front, a social upheaval of a different sort continued. The inland portion of the United States had been explored and opened up on the back of a horse, and its fertile farmlands had been tamed behind a horse and plow. But that way of life was fast disappearing in favor of new technologies and mechanization. Henry Ford had introduced the first mass-produced tractor—the Fordson—in 1917, and by 1923 it had captured 77 percent of the U.S. market.

While these earth-shaking events would one day dramatically impact his life, to one lanky teen-aged farm boy who sat in the stands at Findlay, Ohio's Hancock County fairgrounds, they seemed too far away to worry about.

For him, what mattered at the moment was taking in the sights and sounds of his very first horse show.

Born to Compete

The Buckeye Western Horse Association had been founded on July 10, 1942, with 35 members. One of the first organizations of its kind in the state, its birth was a portent of things to come. The role played by horses and mules in agriculture was in a state of flux. Tractors and combines were the norm now, and horse-driven farm implements were fast disappearing from the rural landscape.

The horse was becoming less of a utilitarian workmate and more of a recreational partner. As a result, saddle clubs and horse show organizations began springing up throughout the country. They were created, so it would seem, with a dual purpose in mind. On the one hand, they served to preserve an ages-old relationship between man and beast; on the other, they explored new forms of horseback competition as a leisure-time pursuit.

As the farm boy watched the participants and their mounts compete against each other in a variety of events, he thought to himself, "I can do this stuff," and vowed to attend the next event as a participant. This he did, and his self-assessment proved to be prophetic.

In short order, the young man established both he and his trick pony "Buck" as a highly competitive tandem. As he later remarked, "We were successful immediately because he [Buck] was broke better than the other horses to do those things."

At the time of the Findlay horse show, President Franklin D. Roosevelt occupied the White House and was the face of the nation during much of the war years. On April 12, 1945—three months into his fourth term in office—Roosevelt passed away and was succeeded by Harry S. Truman.

In stark contrast to Roosevelt's aristocratic demeanor, Truman was a "folksy" man of the people who kept a sign on his desk that read THE BUCK STOPS HERE. As it turned out, that saying also very adequately described the young Ohio farm boy's subsequent life and times.

In President Truman's case, the adage had to do with decision-making and accountability. In the farm boy's case, it had to do with a trick horse named Buck and a horseman's ability to make him and the animals that followed do exactly what he wanted them to. He could, in fact, make Buck go when he wanted him to go and stop when he wanted him to stop.

The farm boy's name was Dale Wilkinson, and this is his story.

THE BUCK STOPS HERE

11

Chapter 1

A Son of the Soil

"I got my first pony as a Christmas present when I was 11. He was big-headed and big-footed, and his name was Buck. . . . I rode him every day of his life."
— **Dale Wilkinson**

Leonard Wilkinson, Dale's father, farmed with horse and mule power.   *Courtesy April Wilkinson Weaver*

Seneca County, Ohio, in the mid-1920s was a land of plenty. Located in the northwestern quadrant of the state and once heavily forested, it had been cleared and converted into highly productive farmland with the help of horses and mules. Now, it and the rest of rural America were in the process of turning away from these four-legged workmates in favor of more-efficient mechanized farm machinery.

And yet the horses remained. No longer *en vogue* as work animals, they were instead being relegated to a more recreational role.

It was into this rapidly changing world that a certain young farm boy was born. It was a world that, while currently basking in the technological, cultural and artistic light of the "Roaring Twenties," would all-too-soon be caught up in the hand-to-mouth dark times of the "Dirty Thirties."

The farm boy would witness these changes—and a host of others, as well. As part of a generation that would live through times of plenty and times of scarcity, times of peace and times of war, he would wind up wearing several different hats—the straw hat of a Midwestern farm boy, the metal helmet of an armed infantryman, and the hard hat of a post-war factory machinist.

In addition, there was one more hat the boy would don. This one had a high crown and wide brim, and it would remain in place the longest. It was a cowboy hat; the kind a horseman wore.

And a horseman was all that Dale Wilkinson ever wanted to be.

In 1936, Leonard Wilkinson bought his 11-year-old son a pony, saddle and bridle for $35.
Courtesy April Wilkinson Weaver

Born to be a Horseman

Dale Eugene Wilkinson was born in Seneca County, Ohio, on August 3, 1925. The youngest child of Leonard L. and Sarah (Lawrence) Wilkinson, he had an older brother named Wayne, born in 1920, and an older sister named Helen, born in 1922.

The Wilkinsons were a typical rural family of that day and age. Leonard was a tenant farmer who worked a small plot of land on shares. He raised wheat as a cash crop, and corn and oats to feed his livestock.

In typical fashion, he also kept a few dual-purpose cows to provide meat, milk, cream and butter; some hogs to provide meat; and a flock of chickens to provide meat and eggs. Any surplus production from the cows and chickens was sold to garner what was commonly known as "butter and egg" money.

In addition to the livestock, the Wilkinson family also planted a garden every spring to provide fresh vegetables for the table during summer and fall, and to be preserved and stored in "root cellars" for consumption during the rest of the year.

1940 Wilkinson family portrait. Front row: Sarah Lawrence Wilkinson and Leonard L. Wilkinson. Back Row: Dale (age 15), Helen (age 18) and Wayne (age 20). **Courtesy Wilkinson Family**

Lucy Wilkinson—Dale's life-long wife and partner—grew up in the same community as her husband. She remains, today, the most knowledgeable person about some of the circumstances surrounding her late husband's upbringing and early introduction to horses.

"Dale is generally listed as being from Tiffin, Ohio," she says, "but his parents' farm was actually much closer to the small town of Melmore; it was located about eight miles south of Tiffin.

"Although Dale's father used draft horses for field work, no one in the family took to horses the way Dale did. As a very young boy, he would sneak out to his uncle's pasture and hitch a few bareback rides on the draft horses. And then Buck came into his life.

"Dale's father acquired Buck in late 1936, as a Christmas present for all three kids. Dale was 11 years old at the time, and he pretty much claimed that pony for his own. His family probably viewed Buck as a life-saving measure that kept Dale away from the draft horse foals in the pasture.

"In stature, Buck was more horse than pony and looked the part," Lucy continues. "He probably had draft horse blood flowing through his veins. I don't know from whom he was purchased, or the training that he had.

"I was not in the big picture at that time; I was just one of the younger kids in the community. Buck was Dale's whole world, and whatever he put into that horse in the way of training apparently worked very well."

Wilkinson himself is on record with regard to that first horse and what he learned from him.

"I got my first pony as a Christmas present when I was 11," he said. "Dad had to scrape together $35 to buy him and a saddle. He was big-headed and big-footed, and his name was Buck. I'd get on him without a bridle and a saddle and do whatever I needed to. I rode him every day of his life."[1]

---

[1]Helena Hill, "He Started it All," *NRHA Reiner*, Dec. 1994, p. 136.

By the end of the year, the pre-teen farm boy had taught his new mount to perform several tricks.
Courtesy April Wilkinson Weaver

By the spring of 1942, 16-year-old Dale had expanded his 8-year-old mount's bag of tricks.
Courtesy April Wilkinson Weaver

Although he might not have been the most striking horse alive, Buck's easy-going demeanor made him a willing and dependable trick horse.
Courtesy April Wilkinson Weaver

While Dale Wilkinson never said how he learned to turn his $35 gift horse into a trick pony, there is one distinct possibility that bears exploring. Moreover, it is one that involves one of the most credible turn-of-the-century "horse clinicians" that the country had ever seen. His name was Jesse Beery.

A Cutting-Edge Clinician

Professor Jesse Beery was born on June 13, 1861, on the family farm located near Pleasant Hill, Ohio. His parents, Enoch and Mary Beery, were farmers, and it was in this environment that their son and his five siblings were raised. Mary Beery died when Jesse was 7.

Eventually, Dale and Buck made the transition from performing tricks to winning at horse shows. In this shot, which was taken in October of 1943, Dale is 18 years old.
Courtesy Wilkinson Family

Jesse found out early in life that he had a natural way, a gift if you will, for controlling animals. Before long, his reputation for training horses, mules and dogs was such that he traveled throughout the nation for 16 years, conducting clinics at fairs, expositions and private gatherings.

In 1905, Beery returned home and founded a school called the "Jesse Beery School of Correspondence in Horsemanship."

In 1908, he authored an eight-volume set of books titled *Prof. Beery's Illustrated Course in Horse Training*. In this extensive treatise—one of the first of its kind—Beery touched on such topics as first lesson to the colt, teaching the command "whoa," hitching up the colt, kicking and balking, shying and running away, bad to shoe, and halter pulling.

In addition, Beery's books had a section devoted to teaching horses to do tricks. Among its topics were teaching a horse to say no, stand on a teeter totter, mount a pedestal, lie down, and sit.

Beery passed away in February of 1945 at the age of 83. So popular and enduring were his horse training contributions that his books and methods are still in use today.

The Probable Protégé

While no actual data has surfaced that confirms beyond a shadow of a doubt that 11-year-old Dale Wilkinson employed Jesse Beery's methods to teach Buck tricks in the mid- to late 1930s, the fact remains that it is not only possible that he did so, but also probable.

In 1936, Beery would have been one of the most renowned horse trainers in the Midwest. The fact that his home lay a mere two hours southwest of Tiffin, Ohio, only increased the chances that young Wilkinson knew of Beery, and might have actually attended one of the older man's clinics.

However Wilkinson acquired the knowledge to train Buck, acquire it he did. And, as a result, Buck became a local celebrity. Not only a dependable riding horse, he was an accomplished trick horse who would sit, lie down, and climb onto a small pedestal on command.

Wilkinson continued to train, ride and exhibit Buck for the next several years. Within a short time, he acquired enough experience, and impressed enough of the local gentry, to begin charging to break and train their horses. The going rate was $35 a month.

"I could probably ride a bronc better than anyone in the area," he said. "I could get a colt broke."[2]

In July of 1941, a group of Western horse enthusiasts in neighboring Hancock County organized a horse show. The excitement generated by this event led the same group to formally organize the Buckeye Western Horse Association on July 10, 1942. Sixteen-year-old Dale Wilkinson sat in the stands during the inaugural 1941 event.

"I went to the show and watched," he said. "Then I went home and said to myself, 'My gosh, I can do all that stuff.' So I went the next time and entered ol' Buck. We were successful immediately because he was broke better than the other horses to do those things. It was financially a success, too. Some weekends I'd win $15 or $20."[3]

By today's standards, $15 or $20 might not seem to be a fair return for a weekend of work. At the time, however, the average wage for a full grown man was around 84 cents an hour, or $33 for a 40-hour week. And, as a rule, farm laborers were paid less.

Soon Wilkinson's expertise with horses had become well-established and he began training for outside customers. Sometimes he kept a horse a whole 30 days; other times merely three or four. As horse shows became more profitable, he took the horses he was training to the shows, paid the small entry fees and then kept the winnings.[4] In his mind, he was well on his way to what would become his life's work.

As Dale gained even more horse training experience, he was able to supplement his income by taking in outside horses. Here he is with one of his charges. **Courtesy NRHA**

Meanwhile, right down the road a destiny of a different kind was in the offing.

Her name was Lucy.

---

[2] Helena Hill, "He Started it All," *NRHA Reiner*, Dec. 1994, p. 136.
[3] Christi L. Huffman, "The Master," *Quarter Horse Journal*, Feb. 1999, p. 42.

[4] Christi L. Huffman, "The Master," *Quarter Horse Journal*, Feb. 1999, p. 42

Chapter 2

PARTNERING UP

"As far as meeting Dale was concerned, I cannot think of any particular event that brought us together. Our families lived in the same farm community and, at some point, our lives simply became entwined."

— *Lucy Wilkinson*

The Girl Next Door

Lucinda Mary Sherman was born in Seneca County, Ohio, on December 27, 1928. The youngest child of Ralph and Mary (Flanders) Sherman, she had two brothers and three sisters—Alice, Helen, Marguerite, Eldon and Dwight. A third brother, Eldridge, died of spinal meningitis and pneumonia in 1921 at the age of 2.

"My father's family can be traced back to Diss, England, in 1433," Lucy Wilkinson says. "And, although he resided on a different

Leonard L. and Sarah (Lawrence) Wilkinson lived in Seneca County, Ohio, and were a typical rural family of that day and age.
Courtesy Wilkinson Family

branch of the tree, the famous American Army general William Tecumseh Sherman was a shirttail relative.

"My mother's family was originally from France. At one point, my mother's father supposedly had a little money and was seemingly involved with a railroad. He moved the family to Sedalia, Missouri, where they lived for a few years. He moved the family of six back to Tiffin, and then proceeded to abandon them. My mother's mother was the only grandparent I ever knew."

Like the Wilkinson clan, who lived 2½ to 3 miles away, the Sherman family were farmers. Ralph Sherman owned a 128-acre farm on which he raised corn, oats, wheat and soybeans. And like all of his neighbors, he maintained a sufficient number of farm animals to meet his family's immediate needs. Timothy and clover hay was put up as feed for the cows and horses.

"We never had a lot of livestock," Lucy says. "We had a few milk cows and probably four draft horses. My father never owned a tractor. Toward the end of the 1930s, his health began to fail him just enough so that trying to keep the farm going became too stressful. My brothers were still too young to take over full responsibility so, in 1940, he sold the farm for $6,200 and we moved into a rental house in nearby Tiffin.

"I spent my first two summers after the move baby-sitting for a farm wife. The house that we rented had been a showplace at one time, so I also helped father with the big yard. Our church was located only one-half mile away, and we attended it regularly.

"Dad found a job driving a feed truck for the local farm bureau, and mom was spending about three days a week helping a sister care for grandma Flanders, whose health had begun to fail. I would take short walks in the woods across from our house—following the tracks our landlady's son made when he gathered sap from the maple trees for making maple sugar, picking wildflowers and talking to the Jesus I had learned about in Sunday School."

When she was still a teenager, Lucy embarked on an adventure that afforded her a much broader view of the country she lived in.

"Just before I was to enter my junior year of high school," she says, "the wife of a young doctor who was doing his residency at Massachusetts General Hospital in Boston asked mom and dad if I could go there and stay with them as their live-in baby-sitter. I had babysat their 2-year-old boy for a few weeks.

"Their apartment was located in Brookline, a small community adjacent to Boston, and I spent my last two years of high school there.

"Letting go was not an easy thing for my parents to do, but it was a chance for me to earn some money for things other than clothes; after all, it paid $10 a week. I got a raise to $15 when the cleaning lady quit because she was scared to death of their English Sheepdog.

Although not in the best shape, this photo shows Leonard and Sarah Wilkinson either at the time of their engagement or of their marriage. **Courtesy Wilkinson Family**

Dale Wilkinson's 1943 high school graduation photo. Within two years, he would be called to serve his country during World War II.

Courtesy Wilkinson Family

"I graduated from high school in 1946, and my sister Alice drove mom to Brookline to attend the ceremony."

Even before embarking on her "grand adventure," Lucy had begun dating a quiet young horseman who lived down the road.

"As far as meeting Dale was concerned," she says, "I cannot think of any particular event that brought us together. Our families lived in the same farm community and, at some point, our lives simply became entwined.

"The European Theater of World War II was going on, and kids were dating at a younger age. The uncertainty of the war and how it would affect us all seemed to force us to grow up quicker.

"To begin with, my brothers knew Dale better than I did. They formed what today would be known as an intramural basketball team, and they played their games in the school gymnasium. Dale was 17 years old and a junior in high school when we began dating. I was 14 and in the eighth grade.

"However, our dates were pretty much confined to school activities and the movies. We could see a black-and-white Western for a quarter. If we wanted to see Technicolor, we had to pay more at the theater across the street. The 'after event' meeting place for kids was Isaly's Ice Cream Store, where we splurged on a milkshake or sundae.

"Dale didn't particularly like my leaving to go to Boston, but as providence would have it, he joined the Army in January of 1945 to avoid the Navy. He knew after we were attacked by Japan that he would be forced to serve somewhere, and he preferred land.

"We wrote to each other often and managed to keep our romance alive. My social life in Boston was generally confined to attending the Friday or Saturday night dances at the YMCA. My girlfriends—Marilyn and Doris—and I would go by bus and then by above-ground streetcar, dance with the boys from all over Boston, and then leave them at Howard Johnson's—the gathering place for kids after dances. We had no special dates.

"Another gathering place closer to the apartments was the local drugstore, where I learned that a milkshake in Ohio was a 'frappe' in Boston. And we waited out the war."

A Call to Arms

By late 1941, or around the time that Dale and Lucy began seeing each other, the war in Europe had heated up. It had begun two years earlier with Nazi Germany's invasion of Poland. By early 1941, Germany had conquered or subdued much of Europe.

In June of 1941, Germany launched an invasion of Russia. While many Americans sympathized with the nations resisting the Nazi onslaught, the overriding sentiment was that the fight was "theirs . . . not ours."

That view changed when, on December 7, 1941, the United States Pacific Fleet stationed in Pearl Harbor, Hawaii, was attacked by the Japanese. More than 2,400 American servicemen were killed that day, and America entered the war.

Back home in Seneca County, Ohio, Dale Wilkinson's idyllic life was about to change. He had graduated from high school in the spring of 1943, and was continuing to help his father on the farm and train horses on the side.

Facing the sobering fact that he would no doubt soon be drafted into the military, Dale made the decision to "get right with God," and was baptized on May 21, 1944. Several months later, Lucy left for the East Coast.

On January 10, 1945, Wilkinson enlisted. Germany surrendered on May 7, 1945. After receiving the first part of his basic training at Camp Walters, Texas, he was re-assigned to New Caledonia, an island in the western Pacific Ocean approximately 930 miles east of Australia, to receive the remainder of his training.

Ironically, though Dale had joined the Army to avoid the Navy and water, he spent much of his service time on a boat.

By this time, America had gained the upper hand in the Pacific, and Japan was basically pinned down at home. It was thought that, for America to achieve complete victory, Japan would have to be invaded. Wilkinson was assigned to the invasion force and was, in fact, en route to a staging area in China when the two atomic bombs were dropped—the first on Hiroshima on August 6, 1945, and the second on Nagasaki three days later.

On August 15, Japan surrendered and the war was over.

The Return Home

"Dale was discharged from the Army on August 22, 1946, at Fort Sheridan, Illinois," Lucy recalls, "and he returned home shortly thereafter. We were together again.

"Dale got a job as a punch press operator on the second shift at the local GE [General Electric] plant, but never gave up on becoming a professional horse trainer. I worked for a time at a bookstore and gift shop, and then got a job as a telephone operator. It was decided that I would stay with my sister Marguerite

Dale entered the Army in January of 1945 and was released from active duty in August of 1946. He is pictured here on the left during his basic training.
Courtesy Wilkinson Family

and her husband, as my phone shift was split hours, which meant putting my dad out to drive me back and forth to town so often.

"Dale and I didn't like being apart after nearly two years of war, so we decided to elope. We drove to Kentucky where we were married on October 18, 1947, in a civil ceremony by a judge in Russell, Kentucky. Another couple stood with us as witnesses.

"We drove back to Columbus, Ohio, where Dale had left his horse, Sweet Sue, at a show. Dale exhibited 'Sue' in the Western pleasure class there, and she placed first. That blue ribbon inspired Dale to tackle the larger shows.

"Some might say our honeymoon was over at that point, but I say it lasted 62½ years."

After getting married in the fall of 1947, Dale and Lucy returned to Seneca County, Ohio. To begin with, they lived with Dale's parents. Eventually they were able to move out on their own.

"We found a barn near Tiffin with stalls and enough ground to train a horse," Lucy

Lucy Sherman graduated from high school in 1946. During her junior and senior years, she was employed as a nanny by a Boston, Massachusetts-based medical doctor.
Courtesy Wilkinson Family

recalls. "The living quarters were not great, and there was no running water. It was little more than a large doghouse that had been converted by the owner for his son and his bride to live in for a short time. We felt that if it was good enough for them, it was good enough for us."

Dale's employment at the GE plant did not mean that his pre-war aspirations to become a full-time horse trainer had been compromised; far from it. The factory job was simply a means to an end. It paid the bills until the horse training business could be successfully launched and grown.

Dale's plan of action called for working through the night at the plant, getting a few hours of sleep whenever and wherever possible, then coming home the following morning to immediately begin riding horses.

"Dale began breaking, training and showing horses in this manner," Lucy says. "He charged $85 a month to train, and before long he had earned enough money to buy a Spiegel's saddle for $120. He'd sleep three or four hours a night; that was enough for him. At this time, we had the horses at the county fairgrounds for a few months.

"Then we discovered we were going to be parents and decided we needed to find a little larger house. That process took awhile, so we stayed with my mom and dad until our son Gary was born on May 13, 1948."

Shortly after the birth of their first child, Dale and Lucy were able to rent a house in Tiffin. At first, Lucy stayed home with Gary. Then, she, too, went to work at the General Electric plant "in order to save up for a down payment on a place of our own."

During this time, the Quarter Horse industry had yet to secure a firm toehold in the Midwest. The Palomino industry, on the other hand, was thriving. The Palomino Horse Association—the original registry for the golden-colored horses—had been incorporated in California in 1936. By the mid- to late 1940s, it sponsored numerous Midwestern shows.

Dale felt that having a Palomino show horse would be good for business, so acquired a young stallion named Caleche, who he later gelded.

Caleche, a 1946 palomino by Millstream Hub and out of Flicka by Millstream Shamrock, was bred by Alvin Worden of Findlay, Ohio. Acquired by the Wilkinsons in late 1947 or early 1948, he went on to become a top halter, Western pleasure and reining horse.

At this time, reining was called the "stock horse" class, and it involved maneuvering through a very basic reining pattern—one figure eight, three sliding stops, two rollbacks and a limited number of spins. In 1948, Wilkinson showed Caleche to grand champion stallion honors and a first place in Western pleasure at the All-American Palomino show in Eaton, Ohio.

"We bought Caleche from a friend who had gone down to Oklahoma and brought him back," Lucy recalls. "Dale fell in love with him. He showed him at halter and in stock horse classes. We sold him to a man in Cincinnati. We paid $900 for him and sold him for $3,000; that was a lot of money in those days."

Caleche was also registered with the AQHA, and his show record reveals that he was owned at one time by Robert Q. Sutherland of Kansas City, Missouri. Shown at the 1952 American Royal in Kansas City, he placed third in all-age geldings and second in reining. He was also a halter-point earner at the Ak-Sar-Ben show in Omaha, Nebraska, and the Kansas State Fair in Hutchinson. His last recorded owner was Doyle Matthews of Bristow, Oklahoma.

In early 1952, the Wilkinsons were able to purchase their first home.

"We found eight acres," Lucy says, "12 miles south of Tiffin, near the small town of Sycamore. We moved in shortly before our daughter Mavis was born on June 26, 1952. She arrived in a hurry. I was only in the hospital for 20 minutes before she made her appearance.

"Life in Sycamore did not last long. The country was in an economic recession, and work at GE was not good; they were laying off workers. So Dale decided to quit. His last paycheck was for $39.

"Prior to Dale turning in his notice at the factory, we happened upon what we thought looked like a good opportunity to lease an expansive training facility in Lancaster, Ohio. So we rented the house in Sycamore and moved when Mavis was 2 months old.

"This did not prove to be a good decision, and we were forced to return north after six months. We were basically penniless by this time. We had sold the Sycamore property, so we prevailed upon Dale's parents and moved back in with them.

"GE had recovered from its brief down periods, so Dale went and asked if he could have his old job back. They consented to re-hire him, and he worked there for an additional six years."

As the 1950s unfolded, Dale Wilkinson stood poised to embark on a career that he had seemingly always known was to be his true calling—that of a full-time horse trainer.

One thousand miles to the southwest, a series of events had either occurred, or would soon do so, that cracked open the door for Wilkinson to pursue his dream. Among those events were a devastating drought and a date with some shows for "registered" horses.

This rare photo of Lucy, and the renowned trick horse Buck, was taken either shortly before or after she and Dale were married.
Courtesy Wilkinson Family

Chapter 3

IN FROM THE RANGE

The Texas drought of the 1950s dispersed top-notch Quarter Horses to all points west, north and east, and the breed flourished in ways never before seen

The birth and early growth of the NCHA had a profound effect on Dale Wilkinson's training philosophy. King's Pistol, shown here with owner Jim Calhoun in the saddle, was the 1957 NCHA World Champion Cutting Horse. This classic shot served as the NCHA's official logo for years. **Courtesy Quarter Horse Journal**

By the early 1950s, Dale Wilkinson was well on his way to becoming one of the better-known horse trainers in the Buckeye State. Although not yet 30, his ability to turn green broncs into finished riding and show mounts was becoming well known.

Meanwhile, in the Southwest, two equine associations had been founded several years earlier that would greatly facilitate Wilkinson's attempts to establish himself as a top-notch showman. They were the American Quarter Horse Association, headquartered in Amarillo, Texas, and the National Cutting Horse Association, headquartered in Fort Worth, Texas.

The AQHA

In March of 1939, Robert M. Denhardt, a young Texas A & M college professor, published an article in *Western Horseman* magazine titled, "The Quarter Horse, Then and Now." The article was a rallying point for a group of people who were interested in forming a Steel Dust— or Quarter Horse—registry.

That same month, Denhardt met with several breeders in Fort Worth during the Southwestern Livestock Exposition and Fat Stock Show in an attempt to gauge the interest in a registry. One year later, on March 14, 1940, J. Goodwin and Anne Hall Goodwin hosted a supper in their Fort Worth home to further discuss the matter.

The following evening, 75 people met at the Fort Worth Club. Stock subscriptions were taken, a constitution and by-laws were adopted, 21 directors were appointed, and the American Quarter Horse Association was born.

In addition, Denhardt was able to rally the support necessary to formally launch the AQHA as a Texas non-profit corporation on April 17, 1940.

At its inception, the AQHA had a distinct Texas flavor. Of the 21 original directors, 15 were from the Lone Star State. These

The AQHA, which also figured prominently in Wilkinson's early training philosophy, was formed in early 1940. Spearheading the movement to form a Steel Dust, or Quarter Horse registry, was a young Texas A & M professor named Robert M. Denhardt.
Courtesy American Quarter Horse Heritage Center & Museum

men were, for the most part, champions of the "bulldog" Quarter Horse; an animal characterized as having "fox ears, bulging jaws, loaded forearms, deep heart, tremendous britches, long for his height – 14 to 14-3 – small feet, ample bone and kind eye."

Upset by what they viewed as an attempt by a group of "good ol' boys" to control the fledgling association and thus limit its gene pool and usage, two rival groups were formed.

The American Quarter Racing Association made its debut in January of 1945. It was founded in southern Arizona by Jim Haskell and a small group of Quarter racehorse men.

Cutting was popular long before the formation of the NCHA. In a highly-publicized 1898 contest held during the Cowboy Reunion at Haskell, Texas, "Hub" and owner/rider Sam Graves earned the $150 first-place prize money.

Courtesy **Cutting Horse Chatter**

Not a blood registry, this association's main purpose was to identify horses for racing and devise a uniform method by which their performance could be graded.

The National Quarter Horse Breeders Association was launched in December of 1945, and could count among its members such legendary breeders as Ott Adams and George Clegg of Alice, Texas. In April of 1946, the new organization began the publication of a magazine, The Quarter Horse. AQHA, by contrast, did not launch the Quarter Horse Journal until September of 1949.

For several years, the AQHA, AQRA and NQHBA vied with each other for members and horses. Then, calmer heads prevailed and an agreement was reached on November 13, 1949, that resulted in the merger of all the organizations under the umbrella of the AQHA. This move, orchestrated in large part by then-AQHA President Albert K. Mitchell, removed the last of the political roadblocks and allowed the breed to flourish.

The NCHA

During the era of the open range, cattle from one outfit often drifted and mingled with those of other outfits. Twice a year, in the spring and the fall, neighboring ranchers would join in a roundup to sort out their brands.

Every outfit traveled with a remuda of horses. Within the remuda, each cowboy had a string of horses, some of them more suitable for one job than another. For instance, a cowhand needed a steady mount to patrol the herd during the night, but in the morning he could ride last year's bronc to the far reaches of the roundup circle.

The cutting horse was an elite member of the remuda. A typical cutting horse might have started out in a cowboy's string, but his sensitivity to cattle brought him to the attention of the roundup boss. He was the horse that pricked his ears toward a cow and followed her with his eyes. He instinctively knew not to crowd her, yet was wary of her every move. He made the difficult job of separating cattle easier and quicker. He even made it fun.

Like Quarter Horses—or "Billy Horses" or "Steel Dust Horses," if you prefer—cutting horses had been around for centuries as indispensable tools in the cattle trade.

The first advertised cutting contest was held at the 1898 Cowboy Reunion in Haskell, Texas. Fifteen thousand people, lured by ads in the Dallas News and the Kansas City Star, attended. Because the nearest railroad was 50 miles away, they came on horseback and wagon and hack.

The cutting contest offered a first-place prize of $150, a substantial sum in those days, and 11 riders entered. Old Hub, a horse whose fans swore that he could work blindfolded and without a bridle, was brought out of retirement by Sam Graves for this one event.

The NCHA was formed in 1946. Elected as the new association's first president was Ray Smyth. He is shown here with "Old Paint," one of cutting's first champions.   ***Courtesy* Cutting Horse Chatter**

NATIONAL CUTTING HORSE ASSOCIATION SHOW

Tuesday, Sept. 10th, 1946
8:00 P. M.

DUBLIN, TEXAS
2 DAYS BEFORE DUBLIN RODEO

Purse
HALF OF GATE RECEIPTS ADDED TO PURSE
(Other Half To Dublin Rodeo Association)

PLUS the Entrants Fees of $10.00 and $200.00 added by the National Cutting Horse Association

Entries Close at 4 p. m. Sept. 10th

The National Cutting Horse Association Invites You To Become A Member.

VOLNEY HILDRETH, Sec'y & Treas.
Aledo, Texas

The first NCHA-approved show was held on September 10, 1946, in Dublin, Texas. With a $200-added purse, it attracted many of the Southwest's top cutting horses. **Courtesy Cutting Horse Chatter**

Graves primed the 22-year-old horse with oat mash and prairie hay, and then he tied Old Hub to the back of a wagon and led him all the way to Haskell, a two-day journey. Old Hub would wind up winning the event in grand style, and Graves set aside half of his winnings to ensure that the seasoned campaigner had the best of care for the rest of his days.

The first record of cutting as an arena spectator event was at the Southwestern Exposition and Fat Stock Show in Fort Worth, when a cutting horse exhibition was added to the annual rodeo in 1919. It became a competitive event the following year.

By 1946, there were so many cutting horse contests being held under so many different sets of conditions and rules that a group of 13 cutting horse owners met at the Southwestern Exposition and Fat Stock Show and decided to form an association to establish standard rules and procedures for holding such competitions. Later, at a meeting in Mineral Wells, Texas, the association was incorporated.

The first NCHA-approved show was held in Dublin, Texas, in the fall of 1946. Several years later, Dale Wilkinson began importing performance prospects from Texas to Ohio. He had his eye firmly set on the cutting horse game and, with this in mind, began training Royal King Bailey as a cutter.

Like the AQHA, the NCHA was initially a Texas endeavor. The first NCHA world champion was crowned in 1946. For three years in a row, that honor went to a horse named Benny Binion's Gelding, owned by Binion. Binion hailed from Las Vegas, Nevada, but was a Texan by birth.

Over the next 11 years—from 1949 through 1959—10 of the NCHA world champion cutting horses hailed from the Lone Star State. The sole exception was Snipper W, a Texas-

Benny Binion's Gelding, a 1939 black gelding by Band Time (TB) and out of a Spanish mare, was the NCHA World Champion Cutting Horse for 1946-1948.

Courtesy Cutting Horse Chatter

bred gelding owned and shown to the 1953 title by Don Dodge of Sacramento, California.

Between the years of 1940 and 1950, both the AQHA and the NCHA weathered various and sundry growing pains, and came out stronger organizations. Texas-based as both were, it was always their mission to expand throughout North America. Beginning in December of 1941 and lasting through much of 1945, America was struggling under the wide-ranging shortages brought about by World War II rationing. As a result, little travel was possible, and much of the AQHA's expansion plan had to be put on hold.

Housekeeper, a 1940 brown mare by Westy Jr (TB) and out of an unnamed mare, was the 1949 NCHA World Champion Cutting Horse. ***Courtesy* Cutting Horse Chatter**

After the war was over and travel returned to normal, the association was able to move forward on a country-wide scale once again. Then, as the decade of the 1950s dawned, a devastating natural disaster occurred that accelerated this expansion—the Texas drought.

The Drought

Severe drought began in Texas in 1950. Not confined to the Lone Star State, it quickly spread through the Central Plains and certain Rocky Mountain states. Between the years 1950 and 1957, the lack of rain in Texas easily eclipsed the waterless years of the Great Depression. By the time the drought ended in 1957, 244 of Texas's 254 counties had been declared federal disaster areas.

Put another way, during those eight years there was essentially no grass for the livestock during the summer and no hay for them during the winter.

"As the Association moved into the decade of the 1950s, there was a specter hanging over ranch country. The specter had a name. Government agencies and journalists called it 'drought,' but in ranch country it was 'drouth,' the most dreaded curse on the western range.

"Beginning in 1950 and 1951, it just quit raining all across the Southwest. As the months went by, the curse deepened and spread over a much wider area. Ranchers searched a sun-baked horizon in vain for relief. "The dark clouds did not appear, grass shriveled up and water holes ran dry.

"Men struggled to save their livestock and to hold their creditors at bay. A majority of the most influential AQHA members at this time ran cow outfits, and they were confronting a real disaster. As cattle were shipped off bare pastures in ever increasing numbers, the market collapsed. Still it didn't rain.

Around the time that Dale Wilkinson got seriously interested in cutting horses, Snipper W and Don Dodge (top) and Marion's Girl and Buster Welch were two of the industry's most formidable pairs. Snipper W was the 1953 World Champion Cutting Horse, and Marion's Girl claimed the title in 1954. **Both photos courtesy Quarter Horse Journal**

"Starving cattle and hard-hearted bankers left a man little time, or money, to devote to his horse operation."

As a result of the drought, Quarter Horse dispersal sales became the order of the day and were held on a regular basis. While these dispersals were no doubt devastating to the southwestern Quarter Horse breeders who were forced to hold them, there was one positive outcome for the breed itself. Top breeding and show animals were dispersed to all points west, north and east at an accelerated pace and, once again, the breed flourished in ways never before seen.

Despite the drought, the AQHA itself continued to grow. The first official AQHA show was held at Stamford, Texas, July 2–4, 1940. On August 18, 1952, the AQHA Executive Committee met to establish a new and innovative set of rules through which highly accomplished show horses were to be recognized.

The Highest Honor

In the September 1952 issue of the Quarter Horse Journal, then-editor Willard H. Porter unveiled the results of the special meeting held in Amarillo.

"The combined special meeting," he wrote, "had to do, in the main, with the Register of Merit and the AQHA Championship awards, which were set up in March of 1951 at the annual meeting at Colorado Springs."

To begin with, any AQHA-registered horse that earned one point in a performance event qualified for a Register of Merit; this was later raised to five points. To qualify for an AQHA Championship, a horse had to earn at least 20 points. At least eight of those points had to be won in halter classes and at least eight had to be won in performance contests.

Eighteen months elapsed between the time the ROM and AQHA Championship awards were set up and the first award-winners were recognized. To compensate for this lapse, all

In 1951, the AQHA established a set of rules through which show horses could earn performance Registers of Merit and AQHA Championships. Poco Tivio, a 1947 bay stallion by Poco Bueno and out of Sheilwin, was one of the first horses to earn a Championship. A top NCHA cutting horse as well, he placed fifth in the Top Ten in 1950 and 1951.

Courtesy **Quarter Horse Journal**

points earned by horses between March of 1951 and August of 1952 were tallied retroactively.

In the October 1952 issue of the Quarter Horse Journal, eight horses were named to the initial AQHA Champion rolls—Babe Mac C., J. B. King, Little Egypt, N. R. Paul A, Poco Tivio, Pondora, Snipper W and Star Jack Jr. All eight hailed from west of the Mississippi.

Getting back to Dale Wilkinson and his affinity for cutting horses, six years after the NCHA was launched, the Buckeye State trainer was instrumental in establishing an Ohio state affiliate. On October 5, 1952, the Ohio Cutting Horse Association was founded in Wilkinson's living room after a jackpot cutting.

By this time, Wilkinson had set his sights squarely on the AQHA and NCHA show circuits. To compete successfully at this level, he knew he had to upgrade the quality of his show string.

And this he did.

Royal King, a 1943 sorrel stallion by King P-234 and out of Rocket Lanning, was another great early-day cutting champion. He is shown here with James Boucher after winning the first NCHA-approved cutting contest in Dublin, Texas.

Courtesy Quarter Horse Journal

Miss Nancy Bailey, a 1946 bay mare by Royal King and out of Nancy Bailey, was a five-time NCHA Top Ten finisher. The early successes of the King/Poco Bueno cutting horses no doubt were a factor in Dale Wilkinson's decision to feature the same blood in his early training and showing efforts.

Courtesy Quarter Horse Journal

Chapter 4

MILLSTREAM STABLES

"Now that we were in debt again, we needed to decide what to charge that would draw customers. We settled on $85 per month. Right or wrong, that's what it was."

— **Lucy Wilkinson**

As noted earlier, in the spring of 1952 Dale Wilkinson quit his job at the General Electric plant in Tiffin, Ohio, to more actively pursue his dream of being a full-time horse trainer. When the leased training facility in Lancaster, Ohio, didn't work out, the family returned to Tiffin and Wilkinson resumed working for GE. He continued training horses in his spare time, and even found a way to expand his training opportunities.

"Dale discovered that Frank J. Eggner, a man who owned a horse stables 35 miles

Caliche, a 1946 palomino gelding by Millstream Hub, was one of Dale Wilkinson's first palomino champions.
Courtesy April Weaver

away in Findlay, Ohio, needed to have help breaking some colts," Lucy Wilkinson says. "Mr. Eggner had a regular man who had been with him for a long time and was close to retirement. He did not want this older gentleman working with the younger stock and possibly getting hurt, so Dale drove back and forth seven mornings a week.

"A few months after Dale arrived on the scene, Mr. Eggner decided to buy a second farm and switch his emphasis from horses to Black Angus cattle. The horse facility, which was known as Millstream Stables, was offered for sale. It got its name from the well-known ballad, "Down by the Old Mill Stream," that had been written in 1908 by a local songwriter named Tell Taylor."

A Full-Time Trainer

"In the fall of 1954, we were able to enter into an agreement to buy Millstream Stables," she continues. "The terms of the contract were somewhat unconventional. Our constant moving and the times had drained us financially, but Mr. Eggner was associated with a local bank. He arranged for that bank to finance our loan, and then made a personal loan of $1,000 to us, to use as the down-payment.

"I went to work at the local RCA plant for a time to supplement our income, as we were looking at the necessity of making changes to our living quarters—a small apartment above what had been a vet's office. A carpenter friend came from Dayton and transformed the office and apartment into serviceable living quarters for a young family. Good planning as later on we needed the extra bedroom space for kids who were there to receive instruction as to how best to ride their horses. One of the older ones, Patsy Kelly, actually lived with us like a member of the family for a couple of years. Eventually her mother made it financially possible for Dale to build an indoor arena at our location south of town.

Dale Wilkinson and his son, Gary, out for a circa 1949 or 1950 "pleasure ride" on Caliche. **Courtesy April Weaver**

"Patsy just blended in with our family – playing basketball and kitchen table games with Gary and Mavis. In fact, when April gave warning on a busy Saturday morning (April 8, 1961) that she was going to be arriving, Patsy stayed at the house while I went to the hospital where Dr. Barkey took over. A thoughtful April waited until noon so her dad could come take a peek at her in the nursery and lay eyes on me before I fell totally asleep. (Fathers were not allowed to be in delivery rooms unless there was a problem, and mothers had to stay in hospital several days.)

"Gary had a big backyard to play in with his newfound friends—and under Dale's watchful eye. He was now 5 years old and ready for school, which was within walking distance through the fairgrounds."

"We were fortunate to have a babysitter, Jennie Compton, who was more like a nanny to our kids. Were it not for her, I would not have been able to travel with Dale as much as I did to long-distance shows. She had begun sitting for me when we had just two kids. I would give her enough money to go to the grocery and get what the three of them needed for well-rounded meals. Gary and Mavis were involved in helping with cooking, too. Jennie managed to save some back for a couple of trips to their favorite hamburger shop. Jennie doted on April, and to this day they have a close relationship.

"Gary was 13 years old when April was born and one would think he would not be much interested in her. Boys had their own things to do, but he connected with her. She looked like him. Mavis was the one who had her own thing to do. She had a pony named Shiek in the barn who needed her undivided attention. He had to be ridden, bathed and groomed. Now who did she inherit that from? Must have been Dale.

"When April was about three, she asked Gary where she came from. Now, he was a tease, so he told her we found her sitting in front of the hospital eating a Wilson's hamburger. We did not realize his answer made her think she was adopted. I do not recall that she ever told me she felt that way, but I can understand why. She had quite likely heard stories about Gary and Mavis when they were babies and here she was – big enough to eat a hamburger when we 'found' her. I don't think she suffered any permanent damage. Like Mavis, she inherited the love of horses which grew as she grew and enabled her to encourage Rick in the one facet of this business he was drawn to – training reiners."

Millstream Stables proved to be the perfect place for the Wilkinson family. Situated on only 1.3 acres, it nevertheless had an expansive 24-stall barn. In addition, it was conveniently located next to the county fairgrounds, a facility with a show track that was custom-made for training reining horses. Dale had competed there as a teenager, so he was well acquainted with the lay of the land. All that remained was to build up the business.

"Now that we were in debt again," Lucy says, "we needed to decide what to charge that would draw customers. We decided on $85 per month. Right or wrong, that's what it was.

"This did allow Dale to decide whether to show a horse. He had to be pretty sure of a win, as all expenses were on him, and he kept the winnings. The owners were happy enough to get the trophies and ribbons, and he had return customers. Dale was also able to buy and train some horses and sell them for a good profit, so this time around things began absolutely working out as we hoped they would. Within five years we had our loan paid off."

During his time at Millstream Stables, Dale had many young horsemen who came to work for him. While it is impossible to list everyone, their number included Dave Page, who worked for Dale while in his late teens. He later said, "I was strictly the guy who rode the colts, cleaned the stalls, things like that, but I learned a lot about horses there. I lived at Dale's place, and I was with him 24 hours a day, seven days a week. He mainly specialized in reiners and cutters, and I didn't show for him; I rode the second and third stringers. But he taught me a lot." Dave Page went on to major success showing in AQHA at halter and pleasure.

Any discussion of life at Millstream Stables must include the story of "Brownie", the steer. Gary related that every three or four weeks, Dale would get in a fresh load of cattle to use for cutting training. There was a small lot connected to the barn that was just the perfect size and shape to help horses learn to turn back a cow. Gary states, "In one shipment, there was a steer that simply enjoyed cutting on the horses. He would actually set up the horse and give them a target to learn the moves. That worked out so well that Dale named the steer "Brownie." When the cattle truck backed up to the barn to pick up the cattle, Brownie was the first up the ramp leading all the others. Then, Dale would call to Brownie, 'Hey, Brown, come back here', and Brownie would work his way back through the cattle to the rear of the truck and they would let him out back down the ramp. This went on for many years, with Brownie helping to train numerous cutting horses. Brownie got to be much larger than the rest of the incoming cattle after some time, and Dale had him de-horned so he wouldn't hurt any of the others. With all of Brownie's horse

MILLSTREAM STABLES

M'S QUARTER HORSES

Dr. H. B. Martin   Mabel S. Martin   H. J. Martin

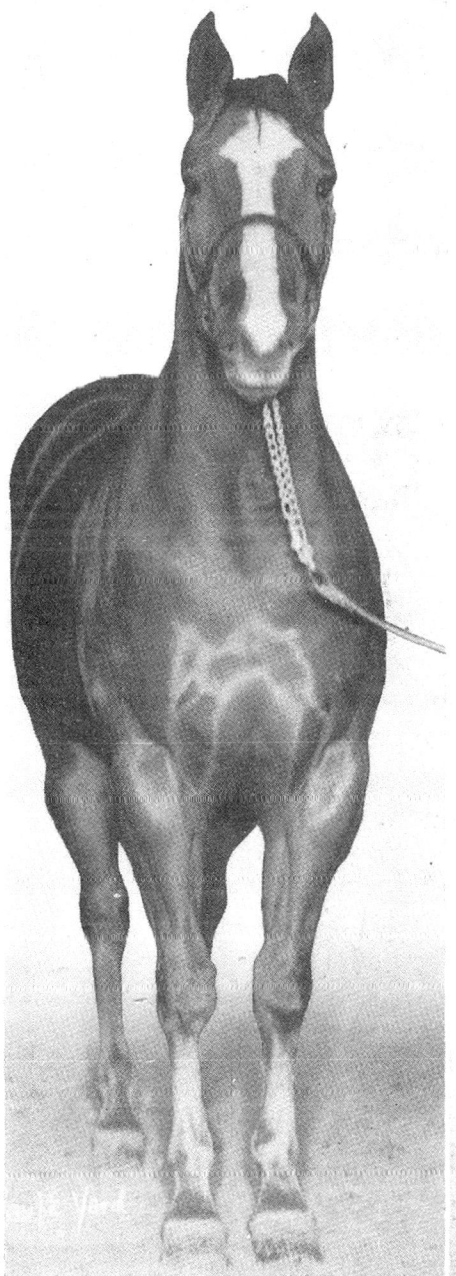

WE have a small but top band of quarter horses, representing the best bloodlines and conformation we can obtain. We are raising some top quality colts and will have young stock for sale from time to time.

Come to See Us

DRUMRIGHT, OKLAHOMA

Ranch located at Junction of State Highways 33 and 99.

M'S DUCHESS 9212   FRED MARTIN 5738

M's Duchess, a 1945 sorrel mare by Chico P 226 and out of Westmoreland, was trained and shown by Dale to her AQHA Championship in September of 1954. The good-looking mare is shown here in an ad placed by her breeders in AQHA Stud Book No. 4 (1948).

training, his feet got to feeling pretty sore, so finally the day came when it was decided Brownie's time at Millstream Stables was done. Everyone gathered in the barn and Brownie lead the cattle up the ramp as usual, but there was no call back from Dale. Working his way back to the rear of the truck, Brownie noticed no open door. Looking down at us all, he began to call. His eyes wide open, he knew something wasn't right. As the truck pulled away, there wasn't a dry eye there that day. If officials kept records, Brownie would be in the NCHA Hall of Fame for all the cutting horses he trained."

During the sometimes stormy Ohio winters, Dale would often go to Texas to show. There he would study other trainers such as Shorty Freeman and Buster Welch. Because Dale felt he would not be taken seriously if people knew he was from Ohio, he first claimed to be from Abilene, Texas. After proving his competency, however, the Texans accepted that he was from Ohio and fondly nicknamed him "O" (as in O for Ohio).[1]

The Wilkinson general "state of the union" was also bolstered by the fact that he now had two legitimate show prospects to be made ready for the AQHA-approved shows that were beginning to crop up throughout the Midwest. The first of these was an Eggner-owned mare by the name of M's Duchess.

The Duchess

M's Duchess, a 1945 sorrel mare by Chico P-226 and out of Westmoreland by Bert, was bred by F. E. "Bob" Weimer of Okmulgee, Oklahoma, and owned at the time of registration by Howard and Mabel Martin of Drumright, Oklahoma.

Chico was a 1936 sorrel stallion by Zantanon and out of Panita by Possum. Bred by Manuel Benavides Volpe of Laredo, Texas—he of King P-234 fame—Chico was owned at the time of registration by Weimer.

Westmoreland, a 1940 bay mare by Bert P-227 and out of an S. Coke Blake mare, was bred by Weimer. One of the top show mares of her era, she earned 18 halter points and was the grand champion mare at the 1951 Kansas State Fair in Hutchinson.

Westmoreland was also a premier producer. Among her six performers were M's Duchess; Monsieur Joe, 1953 AQHA High-Point Halter Horse and Superior Halter; Sutherland's Dwight, AQHA Champion and Superior Halter; and Paulyana, Superior Halter.

While owned by the Martins, "Duchess" was apparently one of the Southwest region's top show mares. AQHA records were, at best, sketchy throughout the 1940s and early 1950s, and thus none of the mare's show winnings from this part of her life appear on her official AQHA record.

In the March-April 1947 issue of *Back in the Saddle*, predecessor to the popular *Horse Lover's* magazine, the following account is given:

"Almost 300 of the top Quarter Horses of the world participated in the Quarter Horse Show of the Southwestern Exposition and Fat Stock Show, Fort Worth, Texas, January 31–February 8. Horses from California, Colorado, Wyoming, Kansas, Oklahoma, New Mexico and Texas took places in this largest of all American Quarter Horse shows.

"The feature [of the show] was the Champion of Champions class, which was for former champions of closed and open shows, one class each for stallions and one for mares. M's Duchess, owned and shown by Howard and Mable Martin, Drumright, Oklahoma, earned Champion of Champion mare honors, after having been named Grand Champion Mare of the regular show."

AQHA records reveal that, by 1949, Duchess had been retired from the show ring and placed in production. On October 24, 1949, the Martins held a production sale that was an absolute record-breaker. The following account of the sale appeared in the December 1949 issue of the *Quarter Horse Journal*:

"The Quarter Horse sale held by Howard J. and Mabel Martin of Drumright, Oklahoma, on October 24, at Pawhuska, Oklahoma, was one of the best this season. Buyers from over the United States attended the sale and the horses were sold to Ohio, Nebraska, Michigan,

---
[1] *NRHA Reiner*, December 1994

Illinois, Kansas and Oklahoma. [The sale averaged] $690 a head on 23 head sold.

"Highlight of the sale was the purchase of the Fort Worth Champion of Champions Mare, M's Duchess, for $5,150. This is believed to be the highest price ever paid for a Quarter mare at public auction. The purchase was made by F. G. Eggner & Son of Findlay, Ohio, owners of the Millstream Stables."

At the time of the sale, Duchess was in foal to Fred Martin, the Martins' senior herd sire. The following year, she produced her first foal, Dutchess Babe, a 1950 sorrel mare.

Eggner's main breeding stallion at the time he acquired Duchess was Phillips 66, a 1937 palomino stallion by Plaudit and out of Miss CS by Tommy Clegg. Bred to this stallion three years in a row, Duchess produced three palomino geldings: Prince Jay (1951), Nan's Tophand (1952) and Mucho Mike (1953).

Shortly after Wilkinson became a Millstream Stables trainer in 1954, he was quick to realize that M's Duchess, broodmare that she was at the time, was an excellent candidate to earn what had become an AQHA Champion award.

The mare happened to be open in 1954, and this no doubt played a part in Wilkinson's decision to show her. By late spring, he had her fit and ready to hit the show trail. Over the next several months, she was exhibited six times—at Indianapolis, Indiana (three times); Columbus, Ohio (twice); and Marion, Ohio.

M's Duchess had earned 10 halter points prior to being placed under Wilkinson's guidance. With him at the helm, she added 11 halter points and eight reining points. She earned her final six points, two at halter and four in reining, at Indianapolis on September 9, 1954. With these points, she was officially recognized as an AQHA Champion and placed back in the Millstream Stables broodmare band.

Our Money—Ohio's first AQHA Champion—was bred by Bob Weimer of Council Hill, Oklahoma, and owned by George Pardi of Cincinnati. M's Duchess was the second. Both were out of daughters of AQHA Hall of Fame Horse Bert P-227.

Getting back to Dale Wilkinson, he was now free to turn his full attention to the horse that would become his first legitimate AQHA superstar—Royal King Bailey.

Midwestern Royalty

Royal King Bailey, a 1951 palomino gelding by Royal King and out of Cricket Bailey by Fred Bailey, was bred by E. E. Blackwood of Comanche, Texas. He was sold as a weanling to Dr. Don Wade of Defiance, Ohio, he of North Wales Farm and Tabano King fame. Dale Wilkinson acquired the then-2-year-old stallion from Wade on March 10, 1953.

Royal King, "Bailey's" sire, was a 1943 sorrel stallion by King P-234 and out of Rocket Laning. Bred by L. A. Lanning of

Royal King Bailey earned his AQHA Championship in August of 1956. Up to that point the versatile performer had earned 13 points in halter, reining, cutting and western riding.

Courtesy **Quarter Horse Journal**

Royal King Bailey, a 1951 palomino gelding by Royal King and out of Cricket Bailey, was acquired by Dale Wilkinson in March of 1953. Here the duo is competing at a Midwestern cutting contest that same year.

Photo by Ralph Crane, courtesy Lucy Wilkinson

Rocksprings, Texas, he was acquired as a yearling by Earl Albin of Comanche.

In a star-studded nine-year show career, the stallion finished in the NCHA Top 10 four times. In 1953, he was the Reserve World Champion Cutting Horse, finishing second to Snipper W and placing ahead of such standout cutting horses as Miss Nancy Bailey, Poco Lena, Jessie James and Skeeter. In 1952, the venerable competitor was third in the standings. In 1954, he ended the year in sixth place, and in 1955, he finished fourth. NCHA records show that Royal King earned Bronze Award No. 42 for winning $10,000, and Silver Award No. 19 for winning $20,000.

AQHA records reveal that Royal King sired 590 registered foals. Of these, 211 were performers that earned three high-point awards, 10 AQHA Championships, 15 Superior awards and 88 performance ROMs. Included among his most notable get were Major King, Miss Nancy Bailey, Royal Jazzy, Royal Chess and Royal King Bailey.[2]

Cricket Bailey, Royal King Bailey's dam, was a 1933 dun mare by Fred Bailey and out of Opal Smith by Barney Lucas. Bred by E. A. Whiteside of Sipe Springs, Texas, "Cricket" was the dam of 12 registered foals and two performers. In addition to Royal King Bailey, she produced Chief Wade, a 1952 palomino stallion by Royal King. In AQHA competition he earned 15 performance points and a Register of Merit. In NCHA contests, he earned $419.11.

After purchasing Bailey in the fall of his yearling year, Dale Wilkinson wasted no time in breaking and training the promising youngster. By the summer of 1953, the Buckeye State horseman had progressed far enough along with Bailey that he was able to give bridleless cutting exhibitions with him.

Shown in Palomino Horse Association

[2] Frank Holmes, *"King P-234 – Cornerstone of an Industry – A Cut Above,"* pp. 124-127

competition, Bailey was the grand champion two years in a row at the All-American Palomino Show in Eaton, Ohio, considered to be one of the largest Palomino shows in the nation at the time. One year, he was entered in eight classes at that show and won them all.

In addition, Wilkinson began hauling his golden show horse to AQHA-approved shows. AQHA records for the period 1953 through 1955 are sketchy at best, but they do show that Bailey competed in 10 approved classes during those three years and earned 11 reining, three cutting and two Western riding points. The palomino no doubt competed in more classes than these, but they do not appear on his official record.

Royal King Bailey's official AQHA record reveals that from 1953 to 1958, he earned 45 cutting points, 22 reining points, 18 halter points and 14 Western riding points. He was awarded a performance ROM in 1953 and his AQHA Championship in 1956.

In an advertisement placed by Wilkinson in the February 1958 issue of the *Quarter Horse Journal*, Royal King Bailey is listed as being the 1955 and 1956 Ohio Cutting Champion. In addition to compiling a solid AQHA show record, he also saw NCHA action and earned $3,823. Gary Wilkinson has fond memories of showing with his dad and Royal King Bailey. He shared this memory: "I remember at Eaton, Ohio, at the Palomino show in 1954 there were two cutting go-rounds and Dale scored 80 for both on Royal King Bailey. At the end of the last go, I was in the stands about 4 or 5 rows up, back under the roof because it was one of those clear and really bright days where the sunshine seemed to penetrate your eyelids. After Dale was announced as the winner, he stepped down and took the bridle off – I had no idea what was going on, but he got back on and Bailey

In the mid-1950s, Dale hauled Royal King Bailey to several of the big Texas stock shows. In 1956, the seasoned pair won the senior reining at the San Antonio Livestock Exposition. **Courtesy Quarter Horse Journal**

REINMAKER

Early on in his show career, Royal King Bailey was shown at halter. Dale and his son Gary are shown with the golden grandson of King P-234 after he had earned grand champion gelding honors at the August 1954 show at Eaton, Ohio. Lucy Wilkinson is in the stands with the Polaroid camera just above Dale's hat. **Courtesy Wilkinson Family**

Dale often worked Royal King Bailey without a bridle – to the amazement of the local crowds. **Courtesy April Weaver**

began slowly walking toward the herd. This all seemed so out of place because I never saw Dale ever work a horse this way at home. Bailey locked onto a cow and out of the herd they came. The palomino glistened bright as gold in the sun, and Bailey's white mane floated weightless in the air. I had to squint my eyes, Bailey was so bright. The crowd was hushed in wonderment of what they were seeing. It seemed the two worked the cow together without a wasted motion and in full control of the moment in time. The backdrop to all of this was the tree-sheltered infield of the track just like a stage – a stoppage in time that I remember like it was yesterday. It was then I understood the passion between man and horse. My eyes still water whenever I think of it."

Meanwhile, the gelding's owner was compiling his own record of sorts.

"During this time period," Lucy Wilkinson says, "Dale was beginning to show quite a few horses and keep their winnings.

"Then, in March of 1959, we sold Royal King Bailey to Tom Hodge Jr. of Fort Worth, Texas, for $5,000, a hefty price at the time. The training, showing and re-sale income, combined with what we got for Royal King Bailey, enabled us to pay off the Millstream Stables note in five years. We felt like we were really on our way."

In the mid-1950s, yet another window of opportunity was opened up to the Wilkinsons. Sonny Braman of Shaker Heights, Ohio, one of Dale's regular customers, decided that he wanted to get in the cutting horse game. On Dale's advice, he purchased a horse named Hollywood Snapper.

A Hollywood Habit

Hollywood Snapper was a 1948 dun stallion by Hollywood Gold and out of Miss Ollie by Tom (Scooter). Bred by the Tom Burnett Cattle Company of Fort Worth, Texas, "Snapper" had been purchased by Dr. D. G. Strole of Abilene, Kansas.

Strole had shown the stallion in AQHA and NCHA competition. In AQHA shows, he earned 57 cutting points and a Superior award. Sold to Braman on December 12, 1955, and turned over to Wilkinson to show, Snapper went on to earn 229 AQHA cutting points. In NCHA competition, he earned $27,858 and was awarded a Certificate of Achievement, a bronze award and a silver award.

In 1958, Snapper was the final horse in the year-end top-10 standings, with $4,206 to his credit. And, in the aforementioned ad that

Hollywood Snapper, a 1948 buckskin stallion by Hollywood Gold and out of Miss Ollie, was trained and shown by Wilkinson to multiple honors in AQHA and NCHA competition. **Courtesy Lucy Wilkinson**

appeared in the February 1958 issue of the *Quarter Horse Journal*, the stallion is listed as being "the grand champion cutting horse of the Ohio Cutting Horse Association and Ohio Quarter Horse Association for the year 1957."

While owned by Strole, Hollywood Snapper was utilized as a herd sire. AQHA records reveal that between 1952 and 1956 he sired eight performers that earned six performance ROMs and four Superior cutting awards. In addition, seven NCHA competitors earned $65,336.84. Snappy Dun, a 1955 red dun gelding out of Miss Ross, was an NCHA Hall of Fame Horse, the 1968 World Champion Cutting Gelding, and the earner of $52,364.

In retrospect, Braman and Wilkinson might have considered leaving Hollywood Snapper intact. With their eyes set firmly on doing well in NCHA competition, however, they gelded him. His last foal crop, numbering three, hit the ground in 1956.

Wilkinson showed Snapper in AQHA competition through August of 1967. In his last contest with Wilkinson in the saddle, the talented gelding placed first in a senior cutting class of eight entries.

In 1967, Braman took Hollywood Snapper back home. Dale Wilkinson was not worried,

Shown in NCHA-approved shows in 1958, "Snapper" finished in the Top Ten. His total NCHA earnings were $27,858.
Photo by Squire Haskins, courtesy Quarter Horse Journal

however. Dating back to the late 1950s, he had discovered that there were worlds of opportunity for an ambitious Midwestern horse trainer who specialized in showing stock horses, or as they are now known – reining horses.

A New Style

As the self-taught horse trainer struggled to care for a growing family, it became apparent to all who watched him ride a horse that he knew secrets not evident to others. His razor-sharp wit and easy rapport with horses and people set Dale apart from the rest. He had an uncanny ability to work with both horses and people. His horses were more fluid and softer, performing with loose reins and flowing maneuvers. They stopped hard, but not as deep as the West Coat horses did. His method of skating a horse across the top of the ground brought the loudest cheers.

"He incorporated the long, sliding stops, flat spins and loose-rein control we see today," Sid Giffith once said. "He started the finesse and style that was a foundation for contemporary trainers." Behind that grace and style were years of observation, experience, natural feel for a horse and unprecedented perfectionism.

"He mentally trained horses, rather than training them to physically do things", Dick Pieper once said. "Dale's lightness and finesse attracted my attention. He had a confident approach to horses. He also had a positive relationship with his horses; there was no jerking or pulling on the reins, which was uncommon at the time." He became a master at getting horses to perform functions with a relaxed attitude using simple, suggestive cues. He was a man of few words, but much wisdom.

Snappy Dun, a 1955 buckskin gelding by Hollywood Snapper and out of Miss Ross, had a star-studded NCHA cutting career.
Photo by Ray, courtesy Cutting Horse Chatter

Chapter 5

A PAIR OF KINGS

"The greatest horse I ever rode – the greatest horse that ever lived – was Rondo's King"

— **Dale Wilkinson**

Dale Wilkinson called Rondo's King "The greatest horse that ever lived."

Photo by Abernathy, courtesy Willkinson Family

At the same time he was deeply involved in the cutting horse game, Dale Wilkinson was also committed to showing reining horses, or "stock horses," as they were then known.

Caleche, Wilkinson's first top palomino show horse, was a western pleasure and stock horse supreme dating back to the late 1940s. Royal King Bailey, his second show ring superstar, was likewise a top cutting and stock horse competitor from the late 1940s through the mid-1950s.

Then, in 1957, Dale Wilkinson began training and showing a sorrel Quarter Horse stallion that would change the very face of the stock horse industry. His name was Rondo's King.

Rondo's King

Rondo's King, a 1954 sorrel stallion by Saltillo and out of Brownie Hargrove by King P 234, was bred by H. F. Hargrove of Uvalde, Texas. Sold as a 2-year-old to Earl Colteryahn Jr. of Bethel Park, Pennsylvania, he was immediately sent to Wilkinson to be trained as a reining horse.

The pair made their show ring debut on June 8, 1957 at Norwalk, Indiana. There, "King" placed second in a field of 12 jr. reining horses. By the end of the year, the Wilkinson-trained 3-year-old stallion had competed in a total of nine reining contests and earned seven firsts, two seconds and 26 points.

Among his most prestigious wins were at the Illinois State Fair, Springfield – first in a class of 29; Chicago International, Chicago – first in a class of 31; and American Royal, Kansas City, Missouri – first in a class of 39. He finished the year as the third high-point reining horse – six points behind Outer's Stubby and three points behind Skipity Scoot.

In 1958, Wilkinson decided to take a crack at the AQHA High-Point Reining Title. Heading out for the winter stock show run in January, Rondo's King placed first at Odessa, Texas; Denver, Colorado; and San Antonio, Texas.

Brought home to the Midwest, he was entered in just four more contests – placing first at Delhi, Ohio; Ak-Sar-Ben, Omaha, Nebraska; State Fair of Texas, Dallas; American Royal, Kansas City, Missouri. The stallion's efforts were enough to earn him the title of AQHA 1958 High-Point Reining Horse.

In later years, Dale Wilkinson was effusive in the praise that he heaped on his "first great reining horse."

"The greatest horse I ever rode – the greatest horse that ever lived – was Rondo's King," Wilkinson recalled. *"He was just great. Rondo's King had a way; an honesty. He had a tremendous desire to run the reining pattern as it*

An excellent win photo of Rondo's King and Dale Wilkinson.
Courtesy Willkinson Family

was at that time. He had such a pleasant way that he excited so many people and taught me so much.

"Our basic standards of training a horse today are exactly what he taught us to do at that time. And anyone who saw him still remembers him. He could ride down that arena right now and out-slide anything; with more balance [and] more charisma. He could outrun them in their circles. The lightness was superb. He was absolutely just a phenomenal horse; ... honest [and] sincere; just a tremendous horse.

"He was a great horse," he continued,

Dale Wilkinson on Rondo's King

Courtesy Wilkinson Family

"because he established what we are trying to do today. A good run today is very similar to what that horse did 30 years ago. After I ran in Chicago with him one time, it was 15 minutes before the next horse could be called into the arena. That was the type of horse he was. I didn't teach him. We allowed him. He just set a standard for us."[1]

One show in particular always stuck out in Wilkinson's mind.

"I won the reining at the Illinois State Fair (in 1958) and they measured his stop at 50 feet," he recalled. *"His distance was unbelievable. His form was exactly the same as the greatest stopping horses today. This thing could stop like a bulldozer. His back was rounded, his hocks were down. I feel we owe him so much for the early direction of the reining horse."*[2]

Unfortunately for owner Colteryahn, trainer Wilkinson and the entire Quarter Horse industry, as good of an athlete as Rondo's King was, he was conversely that poor of a sire. In fact, AQHA records reveal that he sired a mere 10 foals and no performers.

Following close on the heels of Rondo's King into Dale Wilkinson's training facility was a second "King." And this one would prove to be both a top performer and an influential sire. His name was Continental King.

Continental King

Continental King, a 1958 black stallion out of Sue Hunt, is listed as being bred by Ted Clymer of Hudson, Wisconsin. As attested to by Jack Brainard of Aubrey, Texas, the stallion was actually bred by Henry Boehm of La Crosse, Wisconsin.

"In the mid-1950s," said Brainard, "I was training horses in Rochester, Minnesota. Ted Clymer and Henry Boehm were two of my customers.

"Ted Clymer passed away in 1956, and his widow asked me to help disperse the horses. We sold Sue Hunt that year to Henry Boehm, who owned and operated a clothing store called Continental Clothiers.

"Ted Clymer had another top mare that I trained and showed," continued Brainard. "Her name was Martha King, and she was a 1954 chestnut mare by King P-234 and out of Fanny H. When she was a 2-year-old, I showed her at halter at St. Paul, Minnesota. Lloyd Jinkens was the judge, and he placed her first in a class of nine head. The following year, I showed her in the junior reining at Waterloo, Iowa. James Kiser was the judge there, and he placed her first in a class of eight head.

"After Ted Clymer's death, Martha King was put on the market. In the spring of 1958, I called B. F. Phillips, who lived in Frisco, Texas, and told him I knew where there was a good King mare that was for sale.

" 'How much do they want for her?' he asked.

" 'Two thousand dollars,' I said.

" 'Well, I guess I'll take her if you'll agree to haul her down here,' he said.

"So I did. B. F. took her and paid me $100 to deliver her. Then, Matlock Rose went to reining off of her, and she was the 1958 high-point reining mare."

Getting back to Continental King and his real breeder, Jack Brainard had a hand in that, as well.

"After I cut the deal on Martha King," he said, "I called Henry Boehm up and told him that, as long as I had to haul a horse to Texas, he might as well book Sue Hunt to King. I had a two-horse trailer at the time, and couldn't see going that far south with just one horse in it.

"Henry agreed, and I loaded both mares and took off. I dropped Martha King off at the Phillips Ranch and then continued on to Rocksprings, with Sue Hunt. We got her bred to King, and Continental King was the resulting foal.

"He's named after Henry's clothing store."

Because of the distances involved, Sue Hunt was left in Jess Hankins' care to be bred and foaled out. Continental King was born on June 8, 1958.

The fact that the young King son had an exceptionally well-bred dam was a matter of common knowledge. Sue Hunt, a 1942 dun mare by San Siemon and out of Little Sue,

---
[1] *NRHA Reiner*, December 1986, p. 34.
[2] Christi L. Huffman, "The Master," *Quarter Horse Journal*, August, 2002, p. 97.

The illustrious King P-234, sire of Continental King.
Courtesy Quarter Horse Journal

was bred by A. I. Hunt of Tulsa, Oklahoma. A member of one of the breed's greatest early-day "golden crosses," she was a full sister to Black Hawk, Joe Barrett, Sandy Benear, Little Sue II, Little Sue III and San Sue Darks.

Having lost King several months prior and understanding full well the potency of Sue Hunt's pedigree, Hankins called Boehm and tendered an offer for both mare and foal. Boehm declined to sell and enlisted Brainard's help in transporting the pair back north.

When Continental King was a 2-year-old, he was started under saddle. Shown one time during 1961 in western pleasure and once in 1962 at halter, he was sold as a 5-year-old in May of 1963 to Dr. John and Mickey Glenn of Cincinnati, Ohio.

A King's Rein

"I broke the colt as a 2-year-old and felt he had enough athletic ability to maybe make a cutting horse," Brainard says. "Dale Wilkinson down in Findlay, Ohio, was about the best-known trainer in the Midwest at the time. In fact, he was quite a ways ahead of the rest of us as far as working with cutting and reining horses was concerned.

"So I called Dale and asked him if he'd consider taking Continental King for awhile and see what he thought. As I recall – and this goes back almost 40 years – Dale kept him for awhile and then sent him back to us. Then, in the spring of 1963, Dale sold the horse for us to Dr. Jim and Mickie Glenn of Springfield, Ohio. The rest, as they say, is history."

Dr. James Glenn, an oral surgeon, was familiar with the King horses, prior to purchasing Continental King. Dating back to the late 1950s he had owned a daughter of King named Olga Fay who went on to earn an AQHA Superior

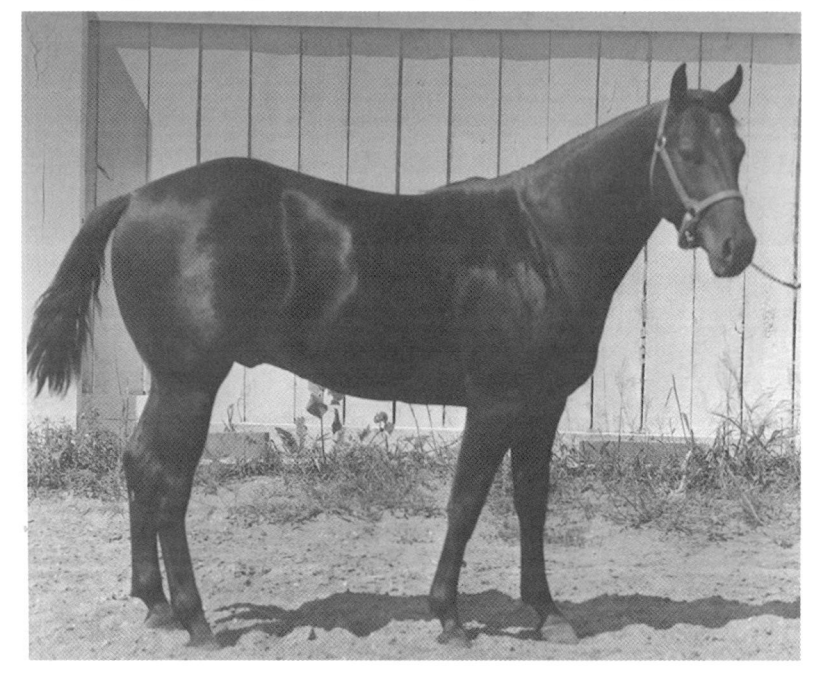

Continental King bears a striking resemblance to his famous sire.
Courtesy Charlie Hutton

Cutting award. Dr Glenn passed away in 1983. His widow Mickie, who currently resides in Hawesville, Kentucky, retains vivid memories of the Continental King years.

"To begin with," she says, "Jim did want Continental King trained as a cutting horse. But Dale was of the opinion that he showed more promise as a reining horse, so that's the path we wound up taking. Dale started out showing him in July of 1964 and did quite well.

"Then, at one show, his assistant trainer Bill Horn took over. It was a little disquieting

Dale Wilkinson on Continental King, who went on to become one of the top reining horses of his era.
Courtesy Wilkinson Family

Continental King was the first horse inducted into the NRHA HAll of Fame. This classic photo of him, with Bill Horm, was the NRHA logo for years. *Photo by Dalco, courtesy* Quarter Horse Journal

for us to see someone else showing our horse – more-or-less unannounced – but Bill did such a good job that we decided that it was going to be all right. From that point on, Bill was King's regular rider and the two forged a partnership that would, in Horn's case, develop into one of the most noteworthy careers in NRHA history.

In the late summer and fall of 1964, Continental King was entered in four AQHA-approved reining classes. The stallion earned two firsts and three seconds, with his most impressive showings being at the Ohio and Pennsylvania state fairs where he placed second in a class of 22 and second in a class of 32 respectively.

With Horn in the saddle, Continental King went on to become one of the top reining horses of his era. AQHA records reveal that, between July of 1965 and September of 1968, the King son was shown in 28 reining classes. Of those, he won 12, placed second 10 times and third six times, earning a Superior reining award and amassing a total of 72.5 performance points (69 reining, two working cow horse and 1.5 Western pleasure).

Among his top wins were the 1965 Indiana State Fair, the 1965 and 1966 Illinois State Fairs, the 1965 and 1966 Ohio State Fairs, and the 1967 Kentucky and Michigan State Fairs.

At the conclusion of the 1967 Midwestern fair season, "Kinger" was retired to stud.

A First-Class Sire

Dating back to when he was owned by Henry Boehm, Continental King had been used as a breeding horse. From the very onset, it was apparent that he was going to be a prepotent sire.

King C Reed, a 1963 brown stallion by Continental King and out of Dimples Reed, was the ex-reining star's first noteworthy performer. Bred by Boehm's Continental Farms in La Crosse, he earned 94 performance points in cutting, Western pleasure, Western riding, trail, hunter under saddle, barrel racing and pole bending.

And, just as LaRue Gooch had discovered years earlier with Easter King, Dr. and Mrs. Glenn were quick to realize that Continental King nicked exceptionally well with the daughters of Hollywood Gold. Among the top performers to result from this cross were:

- Miz Liz Dodson, a 1965 bay mare out of Dodson's Little Star: earner of 42.5 performance points (26 reining, 14 cutting and 2.5 Western pleasure); 1968 NRHA Futurity Reserve Champion; NCHA earner of $2,126.
- Continental Ace, a 1966 black stallion out of Dodson's Little Star: Superior reining; third in the 1969 NRHA Futurity and winner of 23 of 30 AQHA reining classes.
- Continental Buff, a 1966 dun gelding out of Miss Gold 01: Youth Superior reining, NRHA earner of $1,063.

By late 1971, Dr. Glenn's health had begun to deteriorate. In March of 1972,

Miss Liz Dodson, a 1965 bay mare by continental King and out of Dodson's Little Star, was the 1968 NRHA Futurity Reserve Champion.   **Courtesy Quarter Horse Journal**

the decision was made to part company with Continental King by donating him to Ohio State University at Columbus. While under the control of Ohio State University and well-known horseman Charlie Hutton, Continental King continued to establish himself as one of the Midwest's top performance horse sires. Among his top performers during this era were:

- Continental Charo, a 1970 black mare out of Dodson's Little Star: 1973 NRHA Futurity Reserve Champion.
- Clene Continental, a 1972 black gelding out of Mona Weimer: 1975 NRHA Futurity Champion.

In 1975, Charlie Hutton left the Ohio State University to head up the horse program at the University of Georgia at Athens. Several years later, Hutton was able to first lease and then purchase Continental King for the Georgia horse program.

While in Georgia, the King P-234 son finished off his sterling breeding career by siring the following:

- Continental Pistol, a 1979 sorrel gelding out of Gunsmoke Ann: Superior reining; 1989 Youth high-point working cow horse; 1990 Youth high-point reining; Youth Superior reining; earner of 207.5 performance points (75.5 Open, 2.5 Amateur and 129.5 Youth).
- Continental Nancy, a 1982 chestnut mare out of Beauty Bird Kate: 1987 high-point reining and high-point reining mare, Superior reining, earner of 83 performance points.
- King Of Four Mac, a 1985 black stallion out of Nita Joe Wimpy: 1990 high-point reining and high-point senior reining, Superior reining, earner of 124 performance points (116.5 Open and 7.5 Amateur).

Continental King's final siring record was one to be proud of. According to AQHA records, he was the sire of 272 horses. Of these, 59 were performers and they earned two high-point titles, four Superior performance awards and 22 performance ROMs (19 Open and three youth). In addition, they tallied 28 halter and 1,078 performance points (810 Open, 21.5 Amateur and 246.5 Youth). In NCHA and NRHA competition, in an era of low purses they still earned $7,675 and $13,478, respectively.

Continental King was also the maternal grandsire of 181 performers that earned one

Dale showing 1975 NRHA Futurity Champion Clene Continental, a gelding by Continental King. **Courtesy NRHA**

King of Four Mac was the 1990 High Point Reining Horse. Shown by Charlie Hutton, he was also a Superior reining horse and the earner of 124 performance points. **Photo by Dick Waltenberry, courtesy Charlie Hutton**

Amateur world championship, two Amateur high-point titles; 16 Superior performance awards (seven Open, five Amateur and four Youth); and 44 performance ROMs (24 Open, 12 Amateur and eight Youth). In addition, they tallied 27.5 halter and 4,003.5 performance points. In NCHA competition, they earned $266,661, and in NRHA competition, they earned $268,212.

In the spring of 1985, he managed to get yet another mare in foal. By mid-summer, it was apparent that Continental King was nearing the end of his days.

"Even at age 27," Hutton said, "Continental King was remarkably sound on his legs. His teeth were pretty much all gone, though, and he just seemed tired.

"We brought him in and put him in a box stall every night. On the evening of July 24, 1985, he laid down on his side. I knew the end was near, so I stayed with him until around 11 o'clock. Then, my son David, said, 'You go to bed, dad. I'll stay with him and let you know if anything happens.'

"At 2 a.m., David woke me and said, 'He just went to sleep. He never rolled, he never kicked, he just went to sleep and never woke up.'

"So, we had him buried on a little hill overlooking our arena."[3]

In 1988, Continental King was accorded the singular honor of being the first horse inducted into the NRHA Hall of Fame.

As for Dale Wilkinson, the man who had started Continental King on his road to stardom, he was about to enter yet another crucial chapter in his life. As a result of this stage of the renowned horseman's life, he would come to be known as "the father of modern reining."

---
[3] Frank Holmes, "Continental Reign," *King P-234 – Cornerstone of an Industry,"* pp. 215-216

Chapter 6

AN INDUSTRY IS BORN

"I couldn't get the experience of that jackpot reining – the excitement and the enthusiasm – out of my head. I drove back home that evening, determined to do something about it."

— *Marian "Mickie" Glenn*

As noted in previous chapters, the age of specialization within the Quarter Horse industry was spawned with the formation of the American Quarter Racing Association (AQRA) in 1945 and the National Cutting Horse Association (NCHA) in 1948.

After years of slow, steady growth, both the racing and cutting factions launched their own prestigious futurities. Two decades later, the reining horse industry would follow suit.

Prelude to an Industry

The National Reining Horse Association (NRHA) was born in 1966. With the successes of its specialized predecessors available as blueprints, NRHA immediately launched its

Winner of the first NRHA Futurity in 1966, Dale Wilkinson made history aboard Pocorochie Bo, a double-bred King gelding owned by Miles Chester.
Photo by Dalco, courtesy Wilkinson Family

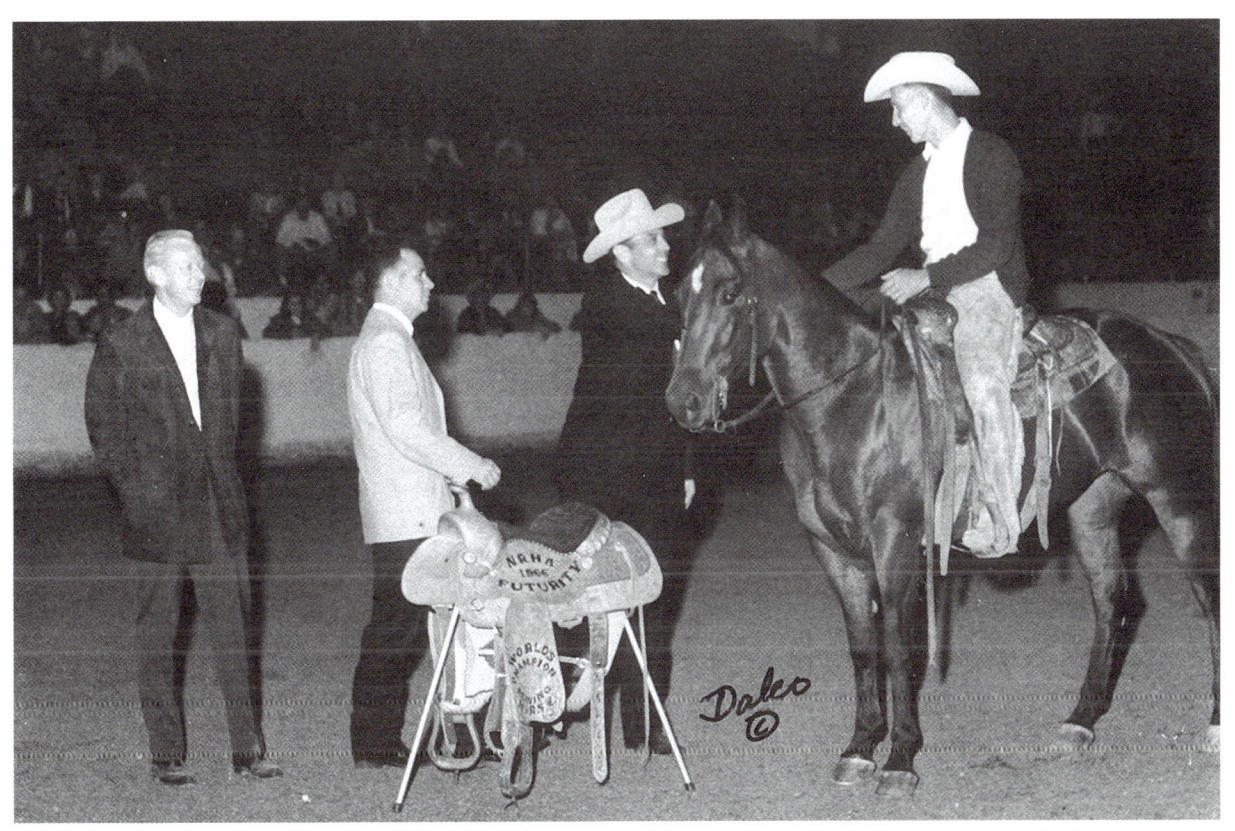

An Industry is Born

Futurity win photo of Pocorochie Bo and Dale Wilkinson   *Photo by Dalco, courtesy Wilkinson Family*

own 3-year-old hallmark event. Like both the racing and cutting futurities, the NRHA extravaganza eventually mushroomed into a $1 million event.

Appropriately enough, Bill Horn and Continental King were instrumental in the birth of the modern-day reining industry.

On October 31, 1965, the team competed in an open reining held at an AQHA show in Dayton, Ohio. Carroll Brumley was the judge and, after seeing the quality of the men and horses entered in the class, he devised a more difficult pattern for them to perform.

Horn and Continental King won the event, and the excitement it generated among owners, riders and spectators alike is credited with setting the wheels in motion that led to the formation of NRHA.

The National Reining Horse Association, as we know it today, stands out as one of the most successful "single discipline" organizations in western horse history. So broad-based and far-reaching is the association in fact, that it might seem far-fetched to assert that it owes its very existence to one single, impromptu show ring contest that occurred more in the mid-1960s.

But so it does. And, as recalled by Mickie Glenn, this lone event had a Dale Wilkinson and Continental King signature on it – from beginning to end.

The Seed is Planted

"To begin with," Glenn says, "my husband Jim wanted Dale to train Continental King as a cutting horse. But Dale was of the opinion that he showed more promise as a reining horse, so that's the path we wound up taking. Dale started out showing him in July of 1964 and did quite well.

"Then, at one show, his assistant trainer Bill Horn took over. It was a little disquieting for us to see someone else showing our horse – more-or-less unannounced – but Bill did such a good job that we decided that it was going to be all right. And, from that point on, Bill was King's regular rider.

"On October 31, 1965, we were at an AQHA show in Dayton, Ohio. Carroll Brumley was the judge and he placed King first in a class of seven sr. reining horses. A lot of the top

57

Midwestern trainers were at the show, and they wanted to have a jackpot reining after all the regular classes were over.

"Carroll said, 'That's fine with me, but I'm going to draw up a different pattern for you to run.' Back in those days, a lot of the reining horse trainers rode all out; they did every maneuver as fast as they could. Carroll seemed to want more control so he had them do their circles at varied speeds – fast and then slow *and under control*.

"I remember that the jackpot was held right at dusk. Most of the crowd had stayed to watch it, and they were whooping and cheering each horse and rider. Continental King and Bill Horn won the class and I couldn't get the experience – the excitement and the enthusiasm – out of my head. I drove back home that evening, determined to do something about it."

And that "something" led to the placing of a phone call to a certain well-known Buckeye State horse trainer.

The NRHA is Born

"After I got home from Dayton," Mickie continues, "I called Dale Wilkinson. I told him about all the excitement that the jackpot reining had generated and asked him if we couldn't plan for an even bigger event just like it, to be held in a year.

"My original thought was that we could all just quit showing for a year, take the money that we would have spent and put it in a pot. Then we could call up some of the 'big boys' and get them to match it. I felt, if we did this, we might wind up holding the biggest jackpot reining of all time. I shared all this with Dale and all he said was, 'Why don't you come up and we'll talk about it.' "

By the mid-1960s, Dale Wilkinson had roughly two decades of showing AQHA cutting and reining horses. And the venerable horseman's experiences with the cutting horse industry would prove to be of the most value to Mickie Glenn and her fellow reining enthusiasts.

In the early 1960s, the National Cutting Horse Association had made the decision to sponsor a three-year-old cutting horse "futurity." It was to be roughly patterned after the Quarter racing futurities that had been in place for decades. Owners would be required to pay a fee to nominate their horses to the cutting futurity, and then supplement that nominating fee with several payments.

The first NCHA Futurity was held on November 23-24, 1962, in Sweetwater, Texas. Forty-seven horses were nominated to it and, of these, 36 actually competed. Up for grabs was

1968 NRHA Futurity Champion, Dudes Blaze, shown by Clark Bradley.
Photo by Dalco, courtesy NRHA

a record purse of $18,375. To put this amount in perspective, consider that Senor George – the 1961 NCHA World Champion – set a new record for money won during a point year when he earned $16,688 in 52 contests.

In the 1962 inaugural futurity, the legendary Peppy San, With Matlock Rose in the saddle, won the semi-finals. Money's Glo and Buster Welch then came back to take the finals, and the over-all championship. The victory was worth $3,828.[1]

In 1965, Wilkinson was well-acquainted with the NCHA and its futurity. And it was exactly this type of "down-the-road" experience that the reining horse industry of that day desperately needed.

"Dale was always such a deep thinker," Mickie says. "So, by the time I got to his place a couple of days later, he had given the matter considerable thought. He told me that my idea was fine, as far as it went – it just didn't go far enough.

" 'What are you going to do after you hold this jackpot reining?,' he asked. Well, I hadn't really thought that far ahead; but he had. 'I think we should form our own association,' he said, 'with our own judging system and our own judges. And I think we should have a futurity for 3-year-old reining horses.'

"By this time, my brain was a little overloaded. 'I can't get anything like that started,' I said. 'Sure you can,' he said. And then he gave me a list of people to call. So, the following Monday, I got on the phone."

1969 Reserve Champion Little Joe Doug & Dale Wilkinson at the NRHA Futurity.
Photo by Dalco, courtesy Wilkinson Family

Over the course of the next several weeks, Mickie Glenn called Zack Wood – the Executive Secretary of the NCHA; and Ronnie Blackwell, the Public Relations Specialist of the AQHA. After completing an initial round of research, she arranged to meet with a group of fellow reining enthusiasts at R. D. Baker's Miracle Water Farm near Dayton, Ohio.

At that historic meeting, the National Reining Horse Association (NRHA) was officially founded, and the decision was made to fund a futurity. Shortly thereafter, the first official NRHA meeting was held in Columbus, Ohio. Among those attending this meeting were Dale Wilkinson, Stretch Bradley, Bill Horn, Jim Cotton and R. D. Baker.

---
1 Frank Holmes, "The Futurity Sire," *King P-234 – Cornerstone of an Industry*, p. 199.

1970 NRHA Futurity Champion Sid Griffith with Red Ants Snort. **Photo by Dalco, courtesy NRHA**

Elected as officers of the newly-formed association were: Dr. James Glenn, President; Stretch Bradley, Executive Vice-President; R. D. Baker, First Vice-President; and Henry Egner, Second Vice President. Executive members were Rodney Vincent and Blair Folck.

The first NRHA Futurity was slated to be held October 6-8, 1966, at the Ohio State Fairgrounds in Columbus. It was to be a $3,000-added event; nominations fees were set at $10 with the total entry fee being $150. Owners were allowed to nominate several horses, but riders were only allowed to exhibit two horses.

The judges for the watershed event were Ronnie Sharpe, John Stutzman and Jack Kyle. Two go-rounds were held on Thursday and Friday, October 6-7; the finals were scheduled for Saturday, October 8. All three scores were to be used to determine the final champion.

Although a tremendous amount of preparation had gone into the planning of the futurity, there were some last-minute obstacles to clear.

An ice hockey game had taken place days before. When approached about removing the ice, the coliseum staff was less than helpful. This did not sit well with Mickie Glenn, the futurity secretary. With signed lease in hand, she tracked down Ohio Governor Rhodes. The ice was removed and proper footing installed.

To further complicate matters, the State Republican Convention was scheduled to be held in the coliseum on the afternoon before the finals. In advance of the convention, the arena floor was covered with green shavings.

"It was a mess," Mickie Glenn recalls. "Everyone was out in force with rakes and shovels to clean the arena floor up; the barn help, hay and feed suppliers, grounds keepers, coliseum crews, owners and riders.[2]

The event offered a total purse of $10,500 and attracted 35 entries. Pocorochie Bo, a 1963 bay gelding by Foolish and out of Poco Baya, won the event – ridden by Dale Wilkinson.

---

[2] Sushil Dulai Wenholz, "34 Years of an American Dream," *NRHA Reiner*, December, 2001, p. 198.

By the time of the futurity, the versatile gelding had already earned an AQHA Championship with points in halter, western riding, working cow horse, trail and reining.

"He was a big stopping horse relative to today," Wilkinson recalled in a 2005 Pat Feuerstein interview. "He was a nice horse, a pretty horse. He didn't take an awful lot of work and he was a kind old horse."[3]

First Command, a 1963 bay stallion by Blue Command and out of L. H. Sally, was the reserve champion. Owned by Dr. M. E. Hays and ridden by Jim Willoughby, he earned $2,050. Rock Paul, a 1963 sorrel stallion by Isis Rock and out of Paulangel, placed third. Owned by Lloyd Hughes and ridden by Bill Horn, he earned $1,000.

Getting back to the event itself, it seemed destined from day one to run in the red.

"To begin with," Mickie Glenn recalls, "we had to rent the facility and put dirt on the arena floor at our expense. Then everyone felt we needed to have some type of entertainment to draw the local crowd in and expose them to our horses. So we hired country western singer

[3] Pat Feuerstein, "The Good Ole Boys," *NRHA Reiner*, August, 2005, p. 36

Del Reeves and paid him $1,400. We ran ads in the local papers and on the radio.

"We decided to also host a $1,500-added cutting to entice the Texans up. Finally, we decided to have an exhibitor party with free food and drink. The bill was outrageous – as much as it had cost to rent the coliseum."

By show's end the fledgling association was $14,000 in the hole. The organizers held a meeting and prepared to "bite the bullet" and kick in enough funds to balance the books. And then R. D. Baker came up with an alternative plan – the Sire & Dam Program.

One of the first of its kind to ever be put into effect, the Sire & Dam Program called on stallion owners to donate stud fees to the association. Under the plan, the owners were afforded the opportunity to promote their stallions; and the association was the beneficiary of a monetary windfall – a windfall large enough to not only balance the books, but move forward on solid financial footing.

As for Dale Wilkinson, the forward-thinking horse trainer, the formation of the NRHA afforded him new opportunities as well. And the Buckeye State native was quick to take advantage of them.

1971 NRHA Futurity Champion, Dupli Katie ridden by Jim Willoughby.   **Photo by Dalco, courtesy NRHA**

Chapter 7

MILLSTREAM SOUTH

"All that was on the acreage when we bought it was an old dairy barn and a small set of corrals and pens. In typical horseman fashion, Dale began renovating the barn before we started building our house."

— *Lucy Wilkinson*

A new start...

As detailed in the previous chapter, Dale and Lucy Wilkinson purchased the original Millstream Stables in the fall of 1954. The Ohio horse trainer and his family enjoyed more than a decade at the facility, from which Dale trained and exhibited some of the Midwestern region's top Quarter Horses.

By 1963, the business had drastically outgrown Millstream's 1.3 acres. Also, as Lucy says, "As interest in cutting horses grew in the Eastern United States, we found ourselves

Millstream South's outside corrals and indoor arena that stalled 24 horses circa 1961.

Courtesy Wilkinson Family

1961 shot of Dale's working cattle. *Courtesy Wilkinson Family*

looking again for a place to accommodate keeping more cattle, knowing, too, that someday the city would not allow them to be kept within city limits. With an eye toward the future, Dale and Lucy purchased two parcels of land totaling 110 acres that were located six miles south of town. Situated adjacent to U.S. route 68, with easy access to three major thoroughfares, the layout was conducive to both immediate and long-range growth.

The new property had previously been owned by a retired doctor and his wife. The original layout consisted of 80 acres and included a spacious colonial-style house. It and four acres, however, were retained by the doctor and his wife.

"All that was on the 76-acre piece of property when we bought it," Lucy Wilkinson says, "was an old dairy barn and a small set of corrals and pens. In typical horseman fashion, Dale began renovating the barn before we started building our house. His first task – and it was a difficult one – was to demolish the concrete dairy stanchions and replace them with box stalls."

While renovating the new property, and continuing to run their training business out of it, the Wilkinsons retained their home in town. Thus began a three-year period of operating both facilities and transferring horses back and forth. Gary was in high school at the time and stayed at the town property until after his high school graduation. He used the Millstream Stables facility to operate a horse boarding program during his high school years, saving for college and then working on the farm during summers while in undergraduate school.

Significant construction was required to create a successful training operation at the farm south of town. Mavis states, "I believe the barn (remodeled dairy barn) had 26 stalls, but they were all different sizes as they had to be fitted around walls and support systems of the barn. There was a clear span area that was left for keeping cattle for cutting. The barn was actually what you would call a bank barn

– it was built into a hill and the top was used for hay storage and tractors, etc.

"Dale also built several turnout pens of various sizes for different uses, along with an outdoor riding pen for cutting and other training. Dale picked this area because the ground had a lot of natural sandy soil to it. It was always a mystery because the rest of the farm had black or clay for dirt. Also there was a barn next to the bank barn that was gutted and used for a tack area and for the farrier when he came. They saved one side which later became a sort of a bunk house. Bill Waterman and Tom McDowell built this. Later, Mike Flarida lived there.

"We had many outdoor riding tracks established. Dale would always ride in different areas trying to find that one spot where horses would ride like they did when he was at the fairgrounds. There was just something about that track that had a great feel to it. He decided on a couple of different areas and made the ground on both tracks a little different from very easy to a little more difficult so a horse had every opportunity to learn to stop." At some point shortly after the purchase, an 80' by 144' indoor arena was built, thanks to support by Patsy Kelly's mother. Several years later an additional 24 stalls were added to the east side of the arena. Several years after that, Dale built a new cattle barn and silo and then a 60-head "tie stall" barn, which was soon turned into a tractor storage/machine barn.

"I know we had right around 50 stalls and it seemed like there were never enough." Mavis states. I can remember having to swap horses out all the time. The majority were Quarter Horses, but there were some Paints and Appaloosas. Dale never turned anything away."

Gary stated that, "The actual physical move out of the Millstream Stables occurred when I was a freshman at Heidelberg College, so I wasn't really involved with it."

Despite not being involved in the actual physical move from town, Gary spent several summers being actively involved in helping to manage the new facility and to maintain the old. His tasks included everything from stall cleaning, hay hauling, fence painting and the myriad of jobs required to keep the farms tidy.

"I would like for one couple to be remembered in Dale's biography. They are Harold and Marie Kelley, a Pennsylvania farm couple who came to work for Dale sometime after we bought the farm at Findlay. I cannot remember the year but what is important is that anyone who ever met them will never forget them. Harold was hired as a farmhand, but he had a horse background. He loved calf roping. He still had pretty good balance when he came to work for Dale, so he was Dale's turn-back man in the cutting arena. His favorite horse was Mr Gun Smoke's first colt who oddly enough could never be completely cured of bucking. He always had to act up occasionally. Harold cherished the challenge. Harold was early to rise and kept busy all day long. At one time, he milked 80 cows – by hand – every day. Dale used to say he and Harold watched Johnny Carson – Dale when he went to bed and Harold when he got up. Dale would tease him about work by asking if he had gotten a certain task done, knowing there hadn't been time for it. Harold would reply with, 'No, I got a busy spell.'

"Birthday parties started before we moved to the country. A farmer lived near Findlay who supplemented his income with what we called truck farm products – watermelon, muskmelon, and corn; they raised the sweet corn. By 8 a.m. at the veggie stand there would be corn that was absolutely fresh. I have had between 50 and 100 people at the party. When it started it was just one of my sisters and her family. It grew. We roasted the sweet corn in little trash baskets or we would take a clean tub and fill it with water for 20 minutes. Then put it on a homemade grill made with concrete blocks and stable front facing (wire). We would leave the husks on. We had hamburger and chicken – upwards of 25 chickens. One year I had 100 chickens.

"For the kids we had a volleyball net. No invitations; we just called people up. Bring a dish if you can."

As his daughter, April, later stated, "Our father was basically a workaholic by most peoples' standards. Working with horses or any type of animal requires many hours of time and devotion, especially to the level of excellence that he expected of himself and others. The physicality of training mixed with long hours didn't lend to too much spare time." April remembers with fondness the annual birthday parties her mother hosted around Dale's birthday in August. After several years, the party grew to numbers of close to 80 -100 with an extended menu. Everybody came, friends, family, customers, fellow horse trainers and people who heard it was a good time. She says, "We would have music and cutthroat volleyball team battles. Dale truly enjoyed it and I think it actually would be "his week" with people coming to ride, visit him, and stay for the party. It was as close to a vacation that he would ever take."

A Training Machine

Dale's daughter, April, once stated that he would be happy if he could ride 1,000 horses a day. That attitude and love of riding carried him to numerous wins in both cutting and reining and ensured that Millstream South would be a success. His methods began with trotting his young horses with very little restraint on their heads. He felt that *"trotting will mellow a horse so that he accepts training, and it teaches him to keep his body straight. Moving in a straight line is the basis for everything we do in reining. The hocks have to go forward—a horse functions off his hocks. The horse's shoulders can't stay up unless the hocks are driving forward. If you are going to do hard things, the hocks need to be straight."*[1]

[1] *NRHA Reiner*, December 1994

Dale caught in a rare moment not on top of a horse, a stocking cap instead of a cowboy hat, taking a break on the steps of the converted dairy barn at Millstream South. circa 1980.

Courtesy Wilkinson Family

The *NRHA Reiner* article also stated, "Wilkinson rides two-handed until he perfects this straight line. Very seldom will he ride circles until the horse can maintain straightness. He explains that once there is control of the shoulder and hip, the mouth will follow. 'If the body isn't functioning, it doesn't matter where the head is'. The trainer's favorite bit is a three-piece broken Bristol. 'I use it more than anything else. It's a bit from which I get discipline and no scare. I do pull on my horses, but it's straight back. Horses will do more with a little reinforcement than they will with sheer love and kindness."

The Mentor

From the beginning, horsemen and women came from all over to learn from Dale Wilkinson, well-known as a master of horse training. Of the many thousands who gained knowledge from Dale, the following are perhaps most significant:

Ronnie Sharpe – NRHA World Champion, NRHA Hall of Fame

Jim Willoughby – 1971 NRHA Open Futurity Champion, NRHA Hall of Fame

Clark Bradley – 1968 and 1974 NRHA Open Futurity Champion, NRHA Hall of Fame

Bill Horn – 1967 1972, 1981 and 1987 NRHA Open Futurity Champion, NRHA Hall of Fame, NRHA's first Million Dollar Rider.

Sid Griffith – 1970 NRHA Open Futurity Champion

Rick Weaver – 1982 NRHA Open Futurity Champion, NRHA World Champion, NRHA President, NRHA Hall of Fame

Todd Crawford – NRCHA Open Futurity Champion, USET Open Reining Champion

Mike Flarida – 1993 and 1996 NRHA Open Futurity Champion, NRHA Hall of Fame, USET Open Reining Champion

Dave Page – trainer of multiple World Champion Quarter Horses

Dale's horse training style transferred easily to people training as well. He wouldn't tell his students what to do, but show them and allow them the opportunity to learn. In an interview in December 1986's NRHA Reiner, Dale commented, "I think, due to the fact I was probably the only person who trained horses for a living back then, everybody came to work for me for a while. I went through a lot of them. It wasn't because I was really hard to get along with, it was just because we were at it a long, long while. I had a lot of good people working for me which I think complements some of the procedures that

1965 AQHA Open Champion Sugar Bar Dell shown by Clark Bradley.
Photo by Dalco, courtesy **NRHA**

we have developed. They all contributed to the procedures, helped develop our association. But most of them – all I taught them to do was work. You'd be surprised what you can do with a horse if you work."

As stated by Sid Griffith in October 2004, "When he rode into the arena, silence fell over the crowd. Everyone had that much respect for him. I don't care who you are. If you're in reining, he's influenced your program somehow", asserts Giffith, who trained and rode for Dale as a teenager after his father purchased Pocorochie Bo. "He never told you how to do things, Griffith said, "He'd give you a road map but you had to navigate it on your own."[2]

Mike Flarida shared his experiences with Dale Wilkinson. "I was fortunate to live only 40 miles or so from him as a kid. When I was a sophomore in High School, I talked to him at Congress and asked if I could work for him the next summer. He asked me what I knew about horses and I said, 'not much'. He asked if knew how to work hard, and I said I knew how to work really hard. He asked if I worked cheap and I said I would work for nothing! Dale said, 'you've got the job'.

"We baled a lot of hay and rode a lot of horses. When I graduated high school I worked for him for a couple years. We started early in the morning, fed, cleaned stalls and went to riding horses – cutters in the mornings and reiners in the afternoons. If hay needed to be baled, we did that, then went back to riding horses. There were no trips to town or laying off; we worked, and we worked hard. He had an unbelievable work ethic and expected it out of others. It was a very disciplined environment with no wasted motions.

"The two biggest assets Dale had were his ability to think in horse terms and to methodically break things down into individual steps. He could take a horse that had a problem with something like a turnaround or stop and break it down into body functions and find out what wasn't working and fix it.

[2] *Western Horseman*, October 2004.

1971 Champion Stake Reining Horse Trodi Command ridden by Jim Willoughby. **Photo by Dalco, courtesy NRHA**

"He taught by example. He didn't say much; all he did was train horses. You had to be observant to pick up what needed to be done. He would let you figure out things and he would watch to see if you were smart enough to get the job done. If you asked what he was doing, he would say something like, 'working on the shoulder', or 'his body isn't aligned.'

"Dale never turned anything away. We rode Standardbreds (trotters and pacers), Morgans, Arabians, Thoroughbreds. I think if someone had asked him to train a yak, he would have said, 'Sure, I got someone that can ride that yak'. There were a lot of horses there. One year I remember we bred 110 mares to Gun Smoke and that was before the days of shipped semen, so they all had to be on the place. So we could have 50 – 75 broodmares there and an additional 60 or 70 training horses plus Dale's horses.

"He was an amazing man and a great rider. He could go to a cutting or reining on Saturday night and beat you and then ride the really bad horses on Monday morning. I saw him ride some really bad horses.

"I am just so grateful that I had the opportunity to work for, and know, Dale Wilkinson. I learned from him how to figure things out and to always work hard. He used to tell me that hard work wouldn't insure success, but you can never be successful without hard work."

In addition to numerous young protégés who came to Dale for guidance, his daughters also learned horsemanship from the best – their dad. Mavis was old enough during the

Mike Flarida credits his early start with Dale Wilkinson for helping achieve a lifetime of reining success.

Photo by Harold Campton

Bill Horn on Trashadaeous, 1990 NRHA Futurity Reserve Champion, 1987 AQHA/APHA son of Be Aech Enterprise and out of Miss White Trash by Mr Gun Smoke. **Photo by Jeff Kirkbride**

earlier days at Millstream South to be a huge help in riding and training along with some future reining and cutting champions. While April was too young in those early days, as she grew, she, too, was able to pitch in and ride with the best of them.

With Millstream South a growing training institution, Dale only needed one more thing – an outstanding horse – to pull it all together, and one was on the horizon.

Todd Crawford on Play Dual Rey, 2010 AQHA Superhorse.
Photo by Dick Waltenberry

Chapter 8

WHERE THERE'S SMOKE...

"I'm glad that I didn't purchase Mr Gun Smoke until he was a 3-year-old. If I'd gotten him any earlier, I'm sure I would have gelded him."

— *Dale Wilkinson*

One year prior to the formation of the NRHA, a Quarter Horse stallion appeared on the Midwestern scene that would dramatically change not only Dale Wilkinson's life, but those of countless other cutting, reining and reined cow horse devotees as well. His name was Mr Gun Smoke.

Bred to Perform

Mr Gun Smoke, a 1961 sorrel stallion by Rondo Leo and out of Kansas Cindy, was bred by Harley and Mamie Price of Bazine, Kansas, and foaled on their farm on April 6.

Rondo Leo, a 1957 sorrel stallion by Leo's Question and out of War Bird, was bred by Dwight Timbers of Glen Elder, Kansas – a cattle rancher, sale barn owner and horse breeder.

As far as his horses were concerned, Timbers was a dyed-in-the-wool racehorse man. In 1950, he had hauled a daughter of Question Mark named Questionaire's Miss to Perry, Oklahoma, to be bred to a promising young sire by the name of Leo. Leo's Question, the resulting foal, was sent to the track and was a consistent AA-rated runner.

After being retired from the track, "Question" was crossed on a number of speed-bred mares including a daughter of

Mr Gun Smoke, a 1961 sorrel stallion by Rondo Leo and out of Kansas Cindy, rose from humble beginnings to become the founder of a great family of arena performers. **Courtesy Wilkinson Family**

War Star AAA named War Bird. Although this "speed on speed" cross was made seven times, it only resulted in one Register of Merit racehorse.

What the cross did produce, instead, was a quartet of full brothers that would all make their mark as arena performers – War Leo, Ace of Limestone, War Olee and Rondo Leo.

War Leo, a 1956 sorrel stallion, was the 1963 AQHA High Point Cutting Stallion and an AQHA Champion with Superiors in halter and cutting. As an NCHA competitor, he was a Top Ten finisher and the earner of $19,749. Rondo Leo, a 1957 sorrel stallion, was an AQHA Champion and the earner of 20 halter and 36 performance points.

Ace of Limestone, a 1960 sorrel stallion, was an AA-rated racehorse, AQHA Champion and the earner of 17 halter and 27 performance points. War Olee, a 1961 sorrel stallion, earned a Superior and 180 points in cutting. As an NCHA performer, he earned $12,190.

Over-all, Leo's Question sired six ROM race horses (three AAA) that earned $53,001; four AQHA Champions and the earners of 14 ROMs, one Superior halter award, three Superior performance awards and 1,068.5 points in all divisions combined. As an NCHA sire, his get amassed earnings of $322,469.

The Leo son's record as a broodmare sire was far more impressive, especially as far as the cutting industry was concerned. NCHA records show him to be the maternal grandsire of the earners of more than $2.6 million.

The top side of Mr Gun Smoke's pedigree, then, was chock full of speed-bred horses that had proved to be equally adept as arena performers. The bottom side was more of the same.

Kansas Cindy, a 1958 sorrel mare by Kansas Star and out of Miss Gun Smoke, was bred by Kenneth Mitchel of Downs, Kansas. Close up in her pedigree she traced to such top race and performance horses as Oklahoma Star, Nowata Star, Walter Merrick's Midnight Jr. and the Haythorn Ranch's Sport.

AQHA records indicate that "Cindy" was bred to Leo's Question as a yearling in 1959. The resulting foal was Leo's Light Foot,

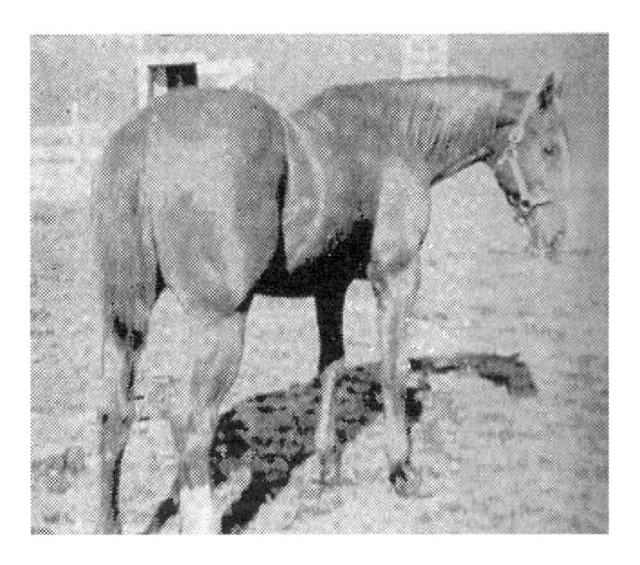

Leo's Question was an AA rated stakes runner on the track. He became a proven sire of halter, race, and performance horses.

Courtesy AQHA

Rondo Leo, a 1957 sorrel stallion by Leo's Question and out of War Bird, was an AQHA Champion with 20 halter, 25 cutting and 11 reining points to his credit.

Courtesy AQHA

Rondo Leo's two full siblings – War Leo (above) and War Otee (right)– were highly successful cutting horses in both AQHA and NCHA competition.

Courtesy **AQHA**

a 1960 sorrel stallion that was the AQHA earner of 37 performance points and the NCHA earner of $1,776.

In mid-1959, both Rondo Leo and Kansas Cindy were acquired by Harley and Mamie Price and the stage was set for the production of Mr Gun Smoke.

The Prices were cattle ranchers and grain farmers who owned a 940-acre Ness County operation in the west central portion of the state. Lifelong partners in every sense of the word, they planted and harvested their crops, and worked their livestock together.

The couple was also avid fans of the American Quarter Horse and, while not well-known on a national scale, were never-the-less capable breeders who took pride in producing the two-way halter and performance horses that were in vogue at the time.

Over the years, their program boasted the close-up blood of such foundation greats as Joe Reed P-3, Oklahoma Star P-6, King P-234, Pretty Boy, and Blackburn.

After purchasing Rondo Leo and Kansas Cindy, the Prices crossed the two for the first time in May of 1960. And it was this mating that resulted in the horse that would end up being the program's most noteworthy contribution to the breed – Mr Gun Smoke.

War Olee earned $12,190.84, an AQHA Superior in Cutting and was third at the 1978 AQHA World Show in Cutting.
Courtesy AQHA

The Rondo Leo/Kansas Cindy cross was made a total of 10 times and resulted in three performers in addition to Mr Gun Smoke: Arlie Leo, 1963 sorrel mare – AQHA earner of three performance points and NCHA earner of $39.45; Price's Smokey Leo, 1973 sorrel stallion by Rondo Leo – AQHA earner of 29 performance points and NCHA earner of $8,408; and Kansas Dillion, 1975 sorrel stallion – NCHA earner of $5,900.

In the fall of 1959, the Prices broke Rondo Leo to ride. "We used him as a ranch horse," Harley said. "He was so outstanding as a using horse and at reining that we decided to have him trained at cutting.

"When he was four years old we took him to Richard Degnan of Ashland, Kansas, for cutting training. Mr. Degnan got him well started and we showed him a few times that year [1961]. The next fall, we took him to Glenn McWhorter of Throckmorton, Texas, to finish."[1]

---
1 Rondo Leo, AQHA Champion profile, *Quarter Horse Journal*, August, 1963, page 46.

AQHA records verify that Rondo Leo was shown at 31 shows between June of 1959 and October of 1963, earning 20 halter points, 25 cutting points and 11 reining points. He qualified as an AQHA Champion on April 8, 1962. The stallion was also shown in NCHA competition and earned $2,744.

Mr Gun Smoke, the first of the Rondo Leo/Kansas Cindy foals to see the light of day, spent much of his early life being shunted from one owner to another.

The Early Years

To begin with, Mr Gun Smoke's breeders did not keep him very long. Whether this had anything to do with the colt's extensive white markings – three high stockings, one half stocking and a wide blaze – or his left blue eye, remains a matter of conjecture. In any event, he was hauled to Fort Smith, Arkansas, at the tender age of five months and consigned to a sale there.

Mr Gun Smoke, shown here with Dale Wilkinson in the saddle, followed in the family footsteps by earning an AQHA Superior Cutting award.

Courtesy Wilkinson Family

It was at this point that fate intervened for the first time when the Leo's Question grandson was purchased for a reported $210 by Bailey "Stretch" Bradley of Hilliard, Ohio. Bradley arranged for the colt to be hauled back to the Buckeye State by fellow horseman Chuck Whitchurch of Vandalia, Ohio.

Whitchurch then proceeded to buy Mr Gun Smoke from Bradley and then re-sell him twice in rapid-fire order – first to Orville Hurst of Dayton, Ohio on September 18; and then to Cletus Fink of Dayton on November 8. Whitchurch was a well-known regional horse trader in those times and one can only guess what the circumstances were that surrounded these two sales and/or trades.

After getting "Smoke" back the second time, Whitchurch kept him for roughly a year before selling him to Bill Nicodemus of New Carlisle, Ohio, on December 23, 1963. Tom Ryan of Weatherford, Texas, was an aspiring young Ohio horse trainer at the time, and Nicodemus' brother-in-law. He vividly remembers this stage of Mr Gun Smoke's life.

"I was at Chuck Whitchurch's place one day, looking at his horses," Ryan says. "Mr Gun Smoke was a long yearling at the time and I kind of liked him. So I called up my brother-in-law and told him, 'I just found a nice registered Quarter Horse colt. I don't have any money, but if you'll buy him, I'll train him and we'll be partners.'

"Chuck wanted $300 for Smoke, so Bill went and borrowed the money from the Reliance Finance Company. His payments on the loan were $25 a month. I broke Smoke as a 2-year-old and tried him out at pleasure and reining. I've seen some accounts over the years that said he was trained as a racehorse as well. I might have goofed around a little just to see how fast he was, but he was never put in any kind of race training and he never saw a track. I did show him once at halter in an open show. He placed last.

"In the spring of Smoke's 3-year-old year, I started him on cattle. Paul Horn was a neighbor of mine and he was trying to be a horse trainer too. Paul had a customer who was a doctor who owned a place near Springfield, Ohio, called Olympic Farms.

"In November of 1961, the doctor had sent Paul down to the big G. B. Howell sale in Seagoville, Texas, in search of a show prospect. Paul wound up giving $8,100 for a weanling son of Leo San named Sanamor. That was more money for a weanling than any of us had ever heard of.

"Anyway, Sanamor was the same age as Smoke, and Paul was going to try to make him into a cutting horse. He had six heifers, but no place to work them; I had a small pen on my place, but no cattle. So I told Paul to bring the heifers up and we'd train the two horses together."

After working Mr Gun Smoke on cattle for a while, Ryan decided that the stallion was showing so much promise that it was time for a more seasoned trainer to take a look at him.

"Dale Wilkinson was about the best-known Quarter Horse trainer in Ohio at the time," he recalls, "so I made arrangements to haul Smoke up to Findlay for him to look at. Bill Horn, Paul's younger brother, was working for Dale at the time. When I unloaded Smoke, Bill was the only one around. He watched me ride the colt around a little and then said, 'Dale will be back in the morning. Why don't you stay the night and let him take a look at your horse tomorrow.'

"So I did. Dale was there the next day and he watched me ride Smoke around. Finally, he said, 'I'd like to keep him here for awhile and see how we get along.' So I left him. A couple of weeks or a month went by, and then my brother-in-law got a training bill in the mail.

"We were a little surprised by this, so we drove up to Findlay. When we got there, we told Dale that we were just a couple of country boys that couldn't afford any training fees. Dale studied on it for awhile and then he said, 'How about if I just buy the colt.' So we dickered back and forth a little and wound up selling him for $2,500.

"Since the horse was in Bill's name, he got the money. I piped up and said, 'Wait a minute; I kept the horse for two years and broke him; what do I get out of the deal?' Dale said, 'My daughter Mae has a nice Royal King mare. I'll breed her to the horse and give you the foal.' And he kept his word. I got a 1967 sorrel filly named Smoked Out that went on to make a top reining horse; in fact, she was the third high point junior reining horse on the 1971 AQHA Honor Roll.

"Mr Gun Smoke was the first registered Quarter Horse Bill and I ever had anything to do with. When we sold him for $2,500, we thought we had the world by the tail. That just goes to show how green we were.

"On the other hand, if we'd kept Mr Gun Smoke, he'd probably have just wound up living out his life somewhere as a back yard horse. Dale was the one who made him famous, so I guess it all worked out for the best."

A Talented Performer

It is worth pointing out that, although Wilkinson took possession of Mr Gun Smoke sometime between the fall of 1963 and the spring of 1964, the ownership transfer was not completed until April of 1967 – three years later.

In any event, the stallion did in fact become a permanent resident of Wilkinson's Mill Stream stables in the mid-1960s. Looking back at the watershed event years later, the venerable trainer admits to having mixed emotions about the stallion. "I'm glad I didn't purchase Mr Gun Smoke until he was a 3-year-old," he said. "If I'd gotten him any earlier, I'm sure I would have gelded him."

In Wilkinson's opinion, Smoke was a gangly, slow-maturing horse that was very

Dale cutting on Marijuana Smoke in the 1978 NCHA Futurity. This son of Mr Gun Smoke was sensitive enough that Dale didn't wear chaps so the leather flapping against his belly area wouldn't distract the colt. **Photo by Dalco**

lightly muscled. In addition, he was so thin-skinned – mentally and physically – that he would almost jump out of his skin when the slightest cue or pressure was applied. As far as the horse's physical abilities were concerned, it was a different story altogether.

"*Mr Gun Smoke was very impressive from the beginning* Wilkinson said. "*He was a very athletic horse, very physical, with a lot of uncontrollable moves. He was also very, very 'cowy.' He could move so fast; too fast. He was really more than you could control.*"[2]

"But once I saw him move, I changed my mind. He was so sensitive that he would react to the lightest cues or pressure. But,

then, as he matured, it all changed. He grew into himself physically and mentally, and became one of the really top competitors."

Once Wilkinson began training Mr Gun Smoke in earnest, he couldn't wait to take him to a show. *Quarter Horse Journal* show results confirm that the stallion was shown in reining at a July 18, 1964, show in Berea, Ohio. There, he placed third in a class of 10 jr. reining horses with R. W. Nicodemus of West Salem, Ohio, listed as his owner.

It was at this point, or shortly thereafter, that Mr Gun Smoke suffered a leg injury. Laid up to recover, the stallion developed ringbone – a malady that persisted over the course of the next several years and one

---
[2] Betsy Lynch, "Mr Gun Smoke, *Legends 3*, p. 171.

that unfortunately caused him to fluctuate between soundness and lameness.

Mr Gun Smoke's official AQHA show record does not make any mention of the 1964 Berea, Ohio, show. Rather, it lists the stallion's first show as occurring at Columbus, Ohio, on September 4, 1966. There, he placed fifth in a class of 24 cutting horses.

Wilkinson hauled Mr Gun Smoke in earnest between March of 1967 and October of 1968.

In 1967, the pair competed in 15 AQHA-sanctioned cutting classes, and earned seven firsts at such places as Columbus, Ohio (twice); Gaston, Indiana; Kentucky State Fair, Louisville; Michigan State Fair, Detroit; Ohio State Fair, and Brantford, Ontario, Canada.

In November, the then-6-year-old stallion closed out the year by placing sixth in a field of 47 sr. cutting horses at the prestigious Chicago International Livestock Exposition, Chicago, Illinois.

Gun Smoke began the 1968 show season by placing fourth in a class of 64 at the huge Southwestern Livestock Exposition & Fat Stock Show, Fort Worth, Texas. Shown twice more that spring and summer, he placed first in a class of 20 at Columbus, Ohio; and third in a class of 21 at La Porte, Indiana.

Sidelined by a busy breeding season, the stallion was rested until the fall of the year. Brought out again in the fall, he won the Indiana, Illinois, Michigan, Ohio and Pennsylvania state fairs. His last outing came in October of 1968 at Columbus, Ohio. There, he placed first in a class of nine registered cutting horses.

Sid Griffith of Columbus, Ohio; and Dick Pieper of Marietta, Oklahoma, were privileged to have seen Mr Gun Smoke in

Smokin 45, a 1982 sorrel stallion by Mr Gun Smoke and out of Lena Dondi by Doc O'Lena, has ROMs in Reining, Western Pleasure and Cutting to his credit. **Photo by Rick Reimann, courtesy AQHA**

action. Both recall him as a different sort of cutting horse.

"[Dale] trained so many great horses," Griffith said, "but I'll always associate him with Mr Gun Smoke. That horse was in a league of his own, because he was so different than other cutting horses of the day. He was so physical and fluid. He covered a cow effortlessly."

Pieper first met Wilkinson in the 1950s while attending Ohio State University, and he later had occasion to watch Mr Gun Smoke perform in the 1960s.

"I remember watching the horse in the mid-1960s," he said. "He was very dramatic with a catty style and a big sweep."[3]

AQHA records attest to the fact that Gun Smoke was entered in 26 registered cutting classes, earning 12 firsts, five seconds, five thirds and a Superior Cutting award with 71 points to his credit. In NCHA competition, he earned $8,476.

It was now time to see what he could do as a sire.

A Sire Serves Notice

Due to the fact that Mr Gun Smoke spent much of the mid-1960s being trained and campaigned as a cutting horse, his career as a sire got off to a decidedly slow start.

Prior to being acquired by Wilkinson, he had sired three foals, and two of them performers: Miss Gun Smoke, 1966 sorrel mare out of Miss Maria – 13 AQHA performance points; and Gunsmokes Ripple, 1966 sorrel mare out of Leading Girl – NCHA earnings of $182.

The stallion's first Wilkinson-era foal crop hit the ground in 1967. Numbering six, it included Smoked Out – the mare that Tom Ryan received in exchange for part of his share in "Smoke;" and Miss White Trash – the line's first legitimate superstar.

Miss White Trash, a 1967 sorrel mare by Mr Gun Smoke and out of Little Miss Hank, was bred by Bill Horn.

"That filly was one of the first horses I ever owned," Horn said. "In fact, Little Miss Hank, her dam, was the first horse I ever owned. I trained and showed Little Miss Hank in cutting for several years, and then, in 1966, I bred her to Mr. Gun Smoke."[4]

As it would turn out, Miss White Trash would go unregistered for the first four years of her life.

"The American Quarter Horse Association wouldn't register the filly because she had too much white," Horn said, "and the American Paint Horse Association wouldn't take her because she didn't have enough. So there I was with a well-bred, well-made filly that no association would accept.

"I told some of my friends, 'No one will register her – they all look at her like she's poor white trash.' So that's what I named her – Miss White Trash. But I knew that wasn't what she was."[5]

Confident of Miss White Trash's potential, Horn decided to point her toward the 1970 NRHA Futurity. Once again, he was told that she was ineligible.

"Unfortunately, the year that Miss White Trash was a 3-year-old," Horn said, "was the only year in the history of the NRHA Futurity that it was open only to registered Quarter Horses. So we were unable to show in it. Both her sire and dam had been good cutting horses, though, so I decided to train her for cutting and enter her in the NCHA Futurity in Fort Worth."[6]

At the futurity, Horn's loud-colored mare placed a respectable fifth in a field of 220. Ironically, she was re-inspected by APHA representatives at the event and accepted into the registry.

---

[3] Jennifer Denison, "Man of Perfection," *Western Horseman*, October 2004, p.59.

[4] Frank Holmes, "One Man's Trash," *Paint Horse Journal*, April 1998, p.68

[5] Frank Holmes, "One Man's Trash," *Paint Horse Journal*, April 1998, p.68

[6] Frank Holmes, "One Man's Trash," *Paint Horse Journal*, April 1998, p.68

Horn continued to show Miss White Trash in NCHA competition for the next several years, and wound up earning more than $10,000. Eventually able to compete in the NRHA, the mare won a number of Open events in that venue and pocketed an additional $13,000 in earnings. Retired to the broodmare band, the colorful cropout would go on to become a noted producer.

Miss White Trash, a 1967 sorrel mare by Mr Gun Smoke and out of Little Miss Hank, went from being a two-breed outcast to becoming an NRHA Hall of Fame Horse.

Photo by T. Becker, courtesy AQHA

Chapter 9

A Smokin' Sire

From an unwanted weanling to a renowned sire whose impact proved to be of great import, Mr Gun Smoke was living proof that color might be skin-deep, but quality goes to the bone.

It is appropriate to remark at this point that Mr Gun Smoke's own coat markings served as an indication that he most definitely was the genetic carrier of a recessive overo Paint Horse color gene. From a historical standpoint, the most logical source of this gene would be the famed Louisiana race mare Della Moore (1912-1930). As the dam of Joe Reed P-3 and Joe Moore P-1856, 'Della' was the cornerstone matron of a family of

Gun Smokes Dream... "I rode her mother and her dad," Wilkinson said. "She was a very fast-moving mare that could read a cow a mile off."
Courtesy NCHA

such consistent color-getting foundation stallions as Joe Reed II, Leo and Hobo.

Wherever the gene came from, there is no doubt that Mr Gun Smoke carried it. Throughout his 20-year breeding career, he sired scores of blazed-faced and stocking-legged get; some were able to be registered with AQHA, while others could only be registered with APHA.

Among the best-known of the Mr Gun Smoke Paint Horses are Docs Gunsmoke, Jester Smoke, Bonnie Smoke and Miss Smokette.

Getting back to Mr Gun Smoke the sire, while Miss White Trash was his first big-time arena performer, she was not to be his last.

By the time the 1967 breeding season rolled around, "Smoke" was in the middle of his abbreviated show career. Many Midwesterners had seen the talented stallion in action and, as a result, brought some good mares to his court. His fourth foal crop numbered 28 and included 15 performers. Among this number was one mare with especially close Wilkinson family ties.

Pana Smoke, a 1968 bay mare by Mr Gun Smoke and out of Pana Dawn by Continental King, was one of her sire's few get to be entered in AQHA competition. Owned and shown by the Wilkinson's youngest daughter, April, the versatile mare earned 13 open halter, one youth halter and 102 youth performance points in six events.

As the decade of the 1960s came to a close, "Gun Smoke's" reputation as a sire grew by leaps and bounds. Helping establish it was yet another pair of marquee performers.

Gun Smoke's Dream, a 1969 bay mare out of Lady Badger 71 by Grey Badger III, was bred by Dale Wilkinson and sold in July of 1971 to Don and Marjorie Padgett of Gahanna, Ohio.

The Padgetts left "Dream" with Wilkinson to be readied for the 1972 NCHA Futurity to be held December 5-10 in Fort Worth, Texas. The Gun Smoke daughter responded by winning the prestigious event over a 248-horse field that included the get of such well-known cutting horse sires as Cutter Bill, Doc Bar, Rey Jay and Gay Bar King.

The total purse of the 11th edition of the winter classic was $120,276. As a result of her winning performance, Gun Smoke's Dream claimed the top prize of $17,839. Shown lightly for the next several years, she had total earners of $20,739.

Hollywood Smoke, the second star of Mr Gun Smoke's "class of '69," was a bay stallion out of Pistol's Holly by Hollywood Pistol. Bred by Bud and Carol Bodell of Lima, Ohio, he had NRHA earnings of $5,809; and NCHA earnings of $1,310. And, like Miss White Trash, he would go on to do his part to enhance the Gun Smoke legacy.

By the mid-1970s, Mr Gun Smoke's reputation as a sire was a matter of fact. So popular was he in the Midwest that news of what his get were accomplishing had reached the West Coast. As a result, the stallion made a one-year sojourn "way out west."

To the Coast and Back (1976-1979)

Greg Ward of Paicines, California, was a top horseman in his own right. As the son-in-law of Dr. and Mrs. Stephen Jensen – they

April Wilkinson and Pana Smoke, circa 1974 or 1975.
Photo by Don Trout, courtesy April Wilkinson Weaver

Debbie Patterson and Gun Smokes Wimpy, a 1984 gelding by Gun Smokes Pistol, won multiple NCHA Non-Pro World Championships. **Courtesy AQHA**

1979 Congress - Bill Horn on Hollywood Smoke, a 1969 son of of Mr Gun Smoke out of Pistol's Holly. **Courtesy April Wilkinson Weaver**

One Gun, the sire of the now infamous Katie Gun.
Courtesy AQHA

of Doc Bar fame – he knew full well the potential worth of an "outcross" stallion such as Mr Gun Smoke.

With this in mind, he contacted Dale Wilkinson and arranged for the stallion to stand the 1975 season in California. Unfortunately, the stallion was not well-received by the Golden State breeders. As a result, he was bred to only a handful of mares and his 1976 foal crop numbered but two.

Among the mares that were bred to the Wilkinson stallion was Janie Bar – one of Doc Bar's first noteworthy daughters. The resulting foal was Smokey Skipjack, a 1976 sorrel stallion that was the NCHA earner of $27,679.

After the discouraging 1975 breeding season was over, Mr Gun Smoke was returned to Findlay, Ohio. There, he stood to a modest book of mares for three years. In retrospect, there were probably two factors that resulted in the lukewarm Midwestern "welcome home" reception.

By this time, the region was heavily populated with Mr Gun Smoke get and grand-get, and the breeders were less inclined to breed to the "head of the stream," and more inclined to look for the next hot cross.

Then too, Mr Gun Smoke had by this time established a track record as a sire of horses with excessive white markings. The fact that the AQHA rules in place at the time barred these horses from registration probably influenced some breeding decisions.

Back on the West Coast, however, a Mr Gun Smoke revival was in the offing, and it was one that would see Dale Wilkinson and his renowned stallion permanently part ways. To begin with, the revival was a result of one talented performer.

Under New Management

Kit's Smoke, a 1973 bay mare by Mr Gun Smoke and out of Mac's Sujo by Fourble Joe, was bred by Laura Bruce of Grayson, Georgia. Purchased in April of 1976 by Benny Guitron and Bert Crane of Merced, California, she went on less than five months later to win the 1976 California Snaffle Bit Futurity.

In 1978, the mare won the NRCHA A division year-end hackamore championship; and the following year, she claimed the 1979 CRCHA Bridle Horse Sweepstakes Championship and the All-Around Stock Horse Contest Championship.

Miss Smokette, a 1968 Sorrel Overo APHA mare, was an APHA Champion with 79 halter points and 32 performance points. **Photo by Roger Graves**

83

Political Smoker won the 1981 CRCHA World Championship Hackamore Maturity. **Courtesy AQHA**

She won every major event she showed in 1979, and became the first horse in CRCHA history to be named as a Supreme Working Cow Horse.

A full sister to Kit's Smoke also made her presence felt on the West Coast. Smokes Belle, a 1974 bay mare, was bred by Laura Bruce of Grayson, Georgia. She was purchased by Pat Hubbert at the 1977 CRCHA Snaffle Bit Futurity Sale for a client. All this, despite the fact that the trainer who rode the bald-faced, blue eyed mare informed Hubbert that the horse "was a little bit crazy."

Hubbert, however, was able to figure "Belle" out, and the pair went on to win many prestigious events, including Salinas, the Cow Palace, Indio, and Imperial. They won the Bridle Class at the Snaffle Bit Futurity twice – in 1980 and 1981. She earned more than $57,000 in reined cow horse competition and – like her older sister Kit's Smoke – was also named as a NRCHA Supreme Working Cow Horse.

As for Hubbert, he liked the "crazy" mare Smokes Belle so much, that he purchased she and her full sister Nuthin But Smoke. "Belle" went on to produce a cropout son by Winnerinic, Smokes Dude, an APHA world champion with Superiors in cutting and reining, also named as an NRCHA Supreme Working Cow Horse.

Pat Hubbert on Smokes Dude, son of Smokes Belle by Winnerinic. **Courtesy NRCHA**

As a result of training and competing with Kit's Smoke, Benny Guitron was now a dyed-in-the-wool "Gun Smoke" fan. After an unsuccessful attempt to talk a group of reined cow horse aficionados into bringing the stallion back to the West Coast, Guitron was able to convince California businessman Gary Wexler to purchase the then 18-year-old stallion in January of 1979.

Mr Gun Smoke took up residence at GW's Futurity Farms near Temecula, under the management of Jeff Oswood.

Coinciding with Smoke's return to the West Coast, several more of his get made highly successful arena debuts. Aledo Smoke won the 1979 California Cutting Horse Futurity; Hol E Smoke was the 1979 RECHA Champion Novice Cutting Horse; and Political Smoker won the 1981 CRCHA World Championship Hackamore Maturity.

The West Coast breeders could not get enough of Mr Gun Smoke. As a result, the stallion's next four foal crops – from 1980 through 1983 – were the largest of his 20-year breeding career. They numbered 56, 84, 74 and 55 respectively.

By 1981, the stallion's stud free had been upped to $5,000. In the fall of 1982, Gary Wexler dispersed his Quarter Horses. Mr Gun Smoke was sold by Wexler to Rapps Quarter Horses of Napa, California, and transferred on September 30, 1982. Rapp owned the now famous stallion through one breeding season and stood him for a fee of $10,000.

Mr Gun Smoke was humanely euthanized on August 11, 1983, due to "leg problems and a recent hip injury" at the age of 22.

From an almost unwanted weanling to a renowned and influential sire whose impact on the cutting, reining and working cow horse industries proved to be of great import, Mr Gun Smoke led an interesting life. He was living proof that color might be skin-deep, but quality goes to the bone.

Smokin Pistol, with Jim Calhoun Jr. in the saddle, was the 1984 AQHA Reserve High Point Performance Horse in Amateur Cutting. He is the sire of many Working Cow Horse performers. ***Courtesy NCHA***

Chapter 10

HIGHER EDUCATION

"Make no mistake about it; Dale Wilkinson was the heart and soul of the University of Findlay's initial horse program – a program that injected much-needed life into the institution."

— **C. Richard Beckett, D.V.M.**
Chair, Board of Trustees

By the mid-1970s, Dale Wilkinson's position as one of the country's top horsemen was secure. Dating back to the mid-1930s, he had been a highly-innovative, highly-successful horse trainer. He had been instrumental in introducing the American Quarter Horse to the Midwest, and had also played a pivotal role in introducing the cutting and reining horse to the same region.

As noted previously, the seasoned competitor had ridden Pocorochie Bo to victory in the inaugural 1966 NRHA Futurity; and had piloted Gunsmokes Dream to the top spot in the 1972 NCHA Futurity.

Construction on Findlay University's "Old Main" building began in 1883, with the college officially opening on September 1, 1886.   ***Courtesy University of Findlay***

Wilkinson's stallion, Mr Gun Smoke, had by now earned a reputation as one of the breed's most promising young sires of arena performers. Both man and horse were, in fact, smack dab in the middle of what would ultimately be Hall of Fame careers. Both were, in other words, "institutions."

In the heart of Findlay, Ohio, there was yet a third institution – a center of higher learning known at the time as Findlay College. In 1974, Wilkinson and Findlay College would join forces to create a truly unique equine center of higher learning – now known as the University of Findlay Equine Studies Program.

As for the host town and its main center of higher education, both were rich in history.

A Colorful Past

Findlay, Ohio, was founded during the War of 1812 that was fought between the United States and Great Britain. Colonel James Findlay built a road to transport troops across the northwestern region of Ohio and constructed a stockade that was named Fort Findlay in his honor. The community of Findlay sprang up around the fort after the war was over.

By the 1840s, there were approximately one hundred families residing in the area. In the mid-1880s, natural gas and oil were discovered nearby and the town experienced rapid growth as a result. In short order, it boasted several newspapers, glass manufacturers, woodworking firms and furniture manufacturers, a woolen mill, brick manufacturers, and a company that made typewriters.

By the time of the 1880 census, Findlay was a bustling town of 4,633 inhabitants. In addition, it was the Hancock County seat – a region that boasted a census-verified population of 27,748.

In early 1882, the "Churches of God in America" and the citizens of the city of Findlay joined together to establish Findlay College "to foster liberal education and christian culture – a Christ-centered college."

Work on the new institution's "Old Main" building began in 1883, with the college officially opening on September 1, 1886. Seventy students held classes on Old Main's third floor while carpenters completed the first and second floors.

As is the case with many small, private schools, Findlay College was more susceptible than the larger, state-supported institutions of higher learning to changes in the national economic and political landscapes.

Catastrophic events such as World War I, the Worldwide Influenza Pandemic of 1918, the Great Depression of the 1930s, World War II and the Korean Conflict all adversely impacted the institution's student body numbers.

In 1938-39, for instance, the college had an enrollment of 317 students. By 1943-1944, and due mostly to WWII massive military conscriptions, the enrollment numbers had dipped to an all-time low of 132. Three years later, the numbers had increased to 474; and by 1967-1968, they reached a high of 1,220 full-time and 236 part-time students.

After experiencing a period of encouraging growth throughout much of the 1950s and 1960s, the college began once again to lose enrollments. By the mid-1970s, the student body numbered a paltry 656 full-time students and it was apparent to all concerned that some innovative tactics had to be adopted in the areas of curriculum and recruitment.

A "shot in the arm" was needed, and it arrived in the form of a quartet of seemingly disparate individuals – a horse trainer, the wife of a college board president, , an academic leader and a veterinarian.

As a member of the foursome who was both a participant and early-day observer of the program, Dr. C. Richard Beckett, DVM, of Findlay, Ohio, recalls the circumstances surrounding one of the most invigorating shots-in-the-arm that Findlay College ever received – the Equestrian Studies Program.

The Doctor and the Horseman

C. Richard Beckett, DVM, was born on April 5, 1935. Clifford and Rebecca Beckett, his parents, owned and operated a 400-acre

Dale Wilkinson with Dr. Beckett at the dedication of Findlay's Dale Wilkinson Arena, August 2005.
Courtesy Wilkinson Family

farm located at Lebanon, Ohio. Dick Beckett grew up with livestock and this no doubt greatly influenced his choice of a career.

After graduating from Lebanon High School in 1953, he attended Ohio State University in Columbus, and earned his veterinarian medicine degree in 1960.

Upon obtaining his doctor of veterinary medicine degree, Beckett then went on to honor a four-year Armed Forces commitment. In 1964, he returned to Ohio and set up his own practice in Findlay. After settling in, he paid a courtesy call to the town's most renowned horse trainer.

"I met Dale Wilkinson the same year I moved to Findlay," Beckett recalls. "I knew who he was when he had his training setup on East Sandusky Street in town. And then, after he moved the operation to the countryside six miles south of town, I decided to pay him a courtesy call.

So I drove in one day to say hello. Dale and a few other people were there. I introduced myself and Dale said, "Yeah...I could use you." That's pretty much all that was said. Our conversation took no more than 15 minutes, after which I left. Then one day I got a call from Dale and the rest, as they say, is history. I was not connected with the college at this time."

The arrival of Dr. Beckett on the scene in 1964 was a timely occurrence because, that same year, Dale's most famous Quarter Horse stallion came to town.

"Mr Gun Smoke came here when he was a 3-year-old," Beckett says. "He was a great horse and a great athlete; I never saw an athlete like him in all of my life. He had ringbone; you could see it coming on as a young horse, and it became more noticeable as he aged. But he had such a big heart and such a desire to perform that it never seemed to slow him down much.

"After Dale had shown 'Smoke' in cutting for a few years, he became an extremely popular breeding horse. We bred him to 100 mares a year; and I practically lived at the farm during breeding season. I was there every other day.

"One year we bred 102 mares and got 93 of them in foal. One day we had 17 mares tied up, wrapped, cleaned and ready to inseminate, and another day we got seven mares in foal at one time.

"And this was in the day before you had all those fancy instruments. It was a wonderful, exciting time around here; a busy time. Dale Wilkinson and Mr Gun Smoke created a lot of interest in this place and, eventually, in Findlay College."

An Equine Education

"We started the [Findlay College] program in 1976," Beckett continues. "It came about through the combined efforts of four people – Joyce Brewer, Dale Wilkinson, Jack McBride and myself."

Joyce Brewer, who can rightfully be given the credit for first suggesting that an equine program of some sort be launched, was the wife of Edward E. Brewer – the President of the Findlay College Board of Trustees.

"Ed and Joyce Brewer had one son and four daughters," Dr. Beckett says. "All of the girls had horses; she boarded them with Dale at his place in town and I was their vet.

The Dale Wilkinson Arena, University of Findlay. *Courtesy University of Findlay*

Dale saw many friends at the dedication of Findlay's Dale Wilkinson Arena. **Courtesy University of Findlay**

"The university was having a difficult time attracting students; it was mostly a business and educational school at the time, with roughly 800 students. Sometime in 1974 – I don't remember exactly when – Joyce came to me and said, 'We have this person here [Dale Wilkinson] with all of this notoriety; why don't we start an equestrian program like the one in Meredith Manor?'

"Meredith Manor was situated in Waverly, West Virginia. It had been started by Ron Meredith in the spring of 1963. At first, it was simply a facility that gave western riding lessons to the public. Then, in 1966 it put a comprehensive equine program together that was designed to teach students the skills necessary to pursue careers within the multi-faceted horse industry.

"Ron and Dale were good friends, so Ron came up here and helped convince Dale that he ought to get involved. This conversation went on for a couple of years. To begin with, I wasn't really that warm to the idea; and I wasn't involved with the university at the time.

"Joyce was undaunted however. Jack McBride was the Vice-President of Academic Affairs at the time and she recruited him to the cause. Glen Rasmussen was the President of the college and he and Dale did not get along – he wouldn't come to the farm to talk to Dale,

Another view of the Dale Wilkinson Arena **Courtesy University of Findlay**

and Dale wouldn't go into town to talk to him. So Jack carried the message and the load to the university. Had it not been for him, we wouldn't have gotten it done.

"By this time, Joyce had also convinced me that this was a project worth pursuing. So Jack and I had perhaps 15 meetings with various components of the institution and people associated with getting a program put together to make it happen. Eventually, it got to the point where the Board of Trustees had to pass it and they did."

Once Dale Wilkinson was convinced that the Findlay College Equestrian Program had potential, he approached it with the same energy and vision that had become the hallmark characteristics of his horse training career. In other words, he didn't sheepishly "test the water;" he jumped in with both feet.

"When it came time to build the facility that we thought we would need for the program," Dr. Beckett says, "the thing that has always stood out in my mind is that Dale took all the financial risk to get it all built.

"He borrowed the money to build a complete, state-of-the art facility that housed a classroom, student lounge, barn managers' office, wash stall, feed rooms and tack lockers. In addition, it contained an expansive indoor arena and a connecting barn with the capacity of housing more than 200 horses.

"Dale went deep into the hole to build the facilities we needed, and he did so on the promise of receiving a stipend for each student and a surcharge of $2,500 above and beyond regular tuition.

"To break even," he continues, "we needed at least 50 students the first year and we had 60. It was another exciting time around here. We didn't know exactly what we were doing or where we were going; we just started.

"Chuck Smith from Ohio State came in and wrote the course outline. He had a master's degree and was in charge. All the students wanted to come here too. It wasn't because of the University of Findlay; it was because of Dale Wilkinson; he was the attraction.

Dale Wilkinson shakes the hand of Clark Bradley, a former competitor and now an instructor at the University of Findlay's horse program. Bradley has been with the college since 1976. **Courtesy Wilkinson Family**

"The first two years it was an associate's degree; not a four-year degree. Then, after two years, we convinced the president that we needed to put a four-year degree together. And that's how we brought Clark Bradley here in 1978 to take the juniors and the seniors.

"Pre-Veterinarian medicine started in 1982; the first year we had seven; the next year we had two. Now it's the largest major at the university – 350 students. The enrollment at Findlay is now roughly 4,000. We have a pharmacy school that has a six-year curriculum; it's a doctorate degree. All of this would have never happened if we wouldn't have had the notoriety for the equine program. The national attention came from everywhere; and all because of one quiet cowboy – Dale Wilkinson."

Cindy Morehead, who has been an instructor in the equine program for over 30 years and is the head coach of the Findlay Equestrian Team, remembers the beginning. She taught equine studies at Meredith Manor in West Virginia for six years. She says, "when they decided to start this program, they came down there to get ideas to put the program together and I was there and I came up here a couple of times to talk about it. Dale's daughter, Mavis, went to Meredith for the nine-month program just to get the feel of the program and what to do and that kind of thing. I also had a cutting horse that Dale had trained, so I would come up here summers and work with Dale and go to shows with them. And then when they started this program, I had left Meredith Manor and Dale called me to come here. So I started second semester of the first year here.

"They had a lot of good kids in the first class, too. I mean like Todd Crawford. Todd is so much like Dale… he kind of looks like him now and he has that same sarcastic humor that Dale had.

"Dale would test people – the day they would come in. I can remember one horse he had named Ranchero. He would stick them on Ranchero and see if they could stay on him, that sort of thing. He would judge people a lot just by how they rode that first time. I mean

University of Findlay Equine students at ISHA May 6, 2012.
Courtesy University of Findlay

A typical University of Findlay Equine Program student.

Courtesy University of Findlay

if you wanted to learn, you could get better. You had to ... for survival.

"I really appreciated the fact that I got to ride horses that he was training, because I did learn to feel what a balanced horse was. I'm so grateful I got to feel that. Sometimes teaching the kids here, you are trying to teach them some feel and what a good horse feels like and some of them have never felt it so it's hard for them to create that feeling in a horse. I thank Dale so much for getting me this job. I feel really lucky to have been able to work here. I have been here over 30 years. It has been my life. I feel like I owe everything to Dale."

It was Dale's unusual combination of training and instructing skills as well as his reputation in the equine industry that drew students to the University's western riding program in its early years. He had a huge impact as a teacher and mentor for such trainers as Ronnie Sharpe, Jim Willoughby, Tom Ryan, Bill Waterman, Tom McDowell, Clark Bradley, Bill Horn, Sid Griffith, Rick Weaver, Todd Crawford, and Mike Flarida.

The equestrian undergraduate program has become one of the largest programs at the university and supports the university's other academic areas because English, science and math are all required in the program's curricula. The program has since expanded to include English Equestrian Studies programs as well as Western. The Equine Business Management Program combines different equine science courses with management topics and traditional business management topics and is designed for students who choose to pursue a career in the equine industry other than the area of training. Currently, equestrian students train more than 350 horses for the public each year. The western program focuses on trail, showmanship, horsemanship, western pleasure, colt breaking, cutting, and reining.

Chapter 11

SOUTHERN COMFORT

Dale Wilkinson had begun to slow down a bit. His lofty position within the over-all western horse industry was secure, as was his reputation as a driving force behind the successful Findlay University equine program.

As he neared his 60th birthday, the legendary horseman made the decision that yet another move was in order – to a more comfortable climate in which he might once again pursue what had initially been his first focus as a trainer.

Mavis "Mae" Garber – Wilkinson's eldest daughter – was privy to exactly what her father's thought process was in considering what would amount to a life-altering "change of climate." Not only was she in on the plot; she agreed wholeheartedly with it.

"By the mid-1980s," Garber says, "Augusta, Georgia was one of the country's most exciting cutting horse hot spots. Much of this was as a result of what has come to be known as the Augusta Cutting Horse Futurity."

The Augusta Attraction

Since the initial event, which was launched as the Atlantic Coast Cutting Horse Association Futurity, the show has grown to feature almost $800,000 in prize money, up from the $726,599 paid out at the 2008 event. The Futurity has $300,000 in added money.

Dale was able to build his Georgia farm from the ground up and enjoyed it for the rest of his life.

Photo courtesy Wilkinson Family

Dale Wilkinson on Peppo Money at the 1986 ACCHA Futurity. — Courtesy Wilkinson Family

Dale Wilkinson on Peppos' Dream at the 1988 NCHA Futurity in Fort Worth, Texas. — **Photo by Don Shugart**

Mavis (Wilkinson) Garber on her 1999 Sorrel Stallion Orphans Got Money.
Photo by Harold Campton, courtesy Mavis Wilkinson-Garber

Over 29 years, the event has drawn 15,290 entries and paid out $15,163,186, including $4.3 million added. In addition to the cutting competition, other activities include the Augusta Stallion Stakes Breeding Auction.

Dale Wilkinson had travelled to Georgia many times to show horses, had customers from that area and knew many people there. He wanted to do more cutting and the Waynesboro area provided this with plenty of pasture to keep cattle, the availability of cattle, white natural sandy soil, along with only having to travel an hour to go to a cutting. So when the University of Findlay made an offer to buy his Ohio farm, he sold it to them and bought ground in Georgia. He was able to build from the ground up to his own specifications. A 30-stall barn was built, along with a separate sizeable hay barn with a shop in one end, and outdoor arenas and pens were added. The barns were completed before the house. Mavis moved into a double-wide home on the property and the Wilkinson's friends, Harold and Marie Kelley, also moved their double-wide onto the property to help.

In early 1984, a large number of horses made the move from Ohio and Dale was set to relax some and just work his own horses. However, when some investments failed little more than a year later, he found himself back to square one, training for the public. Mavis, an excellent trainer in her own right, was a huge help to Dale.

An article in the December 1994 *NRHA* Reiner reported that *"At his age, he continues to break, train and ride horses at his 170-acre facility in Waynesboro, Georgia. 'I'm open for business.' He quipped. His day begins before sunup and concludes at dark. He rides at least 13 customer horses a day. However, it's not without the comfort of a foam rubber pad attached to the*

Mavis and Nick Garber with their son Dakota at his Senior Night football game. **Courtesy Wilkinson Family**

seat of his saddle. 'It keeps my butt from getting sore.' He said, laughing"

As daunting as that schedule sounds, for Dale Wilkinson it was a slow pace. He relied on Mavis and two additional employees to do most of the riding, but he still relished putting the finishing touches on the horses. The *NRHA Reiner* article goes on to say, *"Wilkinson can count on one hand how many days he hasn't been on a horse, which obviously shows in his bowed legs."* His dreams of winning the NRHA or NCHA Futurity were with him to the end.

A typical day for him was a lot like it had been before the move to Georgia. It was back to long hard days, a lot of sweaty saddle pads, going to more shows, showing more, all the late nights in preparing to show. However, when father time started to set in and make it increasingly difficult for his body to do what his mind was so capable of doing, he would work a few cutters and ride a couple of reiners in the morning seven days a week. Dale's afternoons were spent on his golf cart, watching and coaching Mavis.

Dale's competitive side was also apparent at pinochle, a card game he loved to play with his family. Dale always travelled with Nick and Mavis to all the major shows. It gave him a chance to visit with family and friends, particularly the grandkids, Nathan, Sarah and Megan. Dale loved spending time with each and every one of them. Then in 1995 Dakota was born to Nick and Mavis. Having the opportunity to have a grandchild around on a daily basis allowed Dale to enjoy life more. Mavis relates that on one occasion when it was about 100 degrees out, Dale loaded Dakota up in the little farm truck and they headed to town for his first ice cream cone at Dairy Queen. She continues, "When they returned, he pulled up to the barn and said in that slow, quiet voice that we all came to love and knew it was going to be funny, 'Do you know it's hard to eat two ice cream cones at the same time while you're driving?' Dakota had more ice cream on him than in him. Dale continued, 'We probably should have stayed and eaten inside where there was air conditioning.'" Dale loved packing Dakota around on the golf cart, packing picnics and going fishing. Grandma Lucy would fix sandwiches with butter and Vidalia onions. As Dakota got older, Dale seldom missed a football or baseball game. When possible Dale always made time for all the grandkids. They kept him going and young at heart.

As time passed, Dale developed heart problems and had a quadruple bypass in 2005. Later he developed renal artery disease and was on dialysis 3 ½ years. Through it all he continued to think about training and give advice. On a warm sunny February morning, he had ridden and worked cattle on a little mare, "Bobbing For Money", owned by Dr. Johnny Christian, a great neighbour, friend and Dale's primary physician, who made house calls any time day or night. The next day, a fall in the bathroom shattered Dale's hip, he spent three weeks in Intensive Care at a hospital in Augusta, Ga. On March 12, 2010, the Lord called him home.

Dale Wilkinson at the 2005 Futurity Champion Signing
Courtesy Wilkinson Family

Chapter 12

THE LEGEND AND THE LEGACY

A Legend In His Time

The fact that Dale Wilkinson was inducted into the NRHA Hall of Fame, the AQHA Hall of Fame, the NCHA Hall of Fame and the All-American Quarter Horse Congress Hall of Fame clearly identifies him as a Legend. But even more than that, he was a Legend to all of the students, aspiring trainers and horsemen and women who were fortunate enough to know him or watch him ride.

"He's always had an aura about him," said NRHA Past President Dr. Tim Bartlett. "People would wait in line to talk with him or ask him questions. But he also had a great ability to adjust a person's ego. He could pick them up if they were feeling down, or bring them down when it needed to be done. He taught me that there is a lot more to winning than just first place."

A life well-lived is partially reflected in these prestigious awards received by Dale Wilkinson:

1966	Won first NCHA Futurity on Pocorochie Bo
1972	Won NCHA Futurity on Gun Smoke's Dream
1975	Won NRHA Futurity on Clene Continental
1986	First NRHA Hall of Fame Inductee
1988	NCHA Hall of Fame Inductee
1997	Honorary Doctorate for Equine Entrepreneurial Management, University of Findlay
2000	AQHA Hall of Fame Inductee
2001	Received first Zane Schulte Memorial Trainer of the year Award.
2005	University of Findlay's Western Riding Arena designated "the Dale Wilkinson Arena"

The Legacy

As with any truly great horseman, it would be impossible to adequately list all those whose lives were enriched or in some way impacted by Dale Wilkinson. He was a quiet, hard-working, deep-thinking man with strong yet gentle hands. A man who would never tell a person or a horse what to do. He would only suggest or open the door and allow them to figure it out. He was known to awake in the middle of the night with a training idea and get up and go try it out. He understood equine brains in a way unlike most trainers then or since. He didn't believe in forcing the reining or cutting moves necessary, and was one of the first – if not **the** first, to produce long sliding stops without hauling on a horse's mouth. He was a genius in asking and allowing a horse to discover its abilities.

The number of actual Wilkinson protégés will never be known. However, he was constantly surrounded by horsemen and women who hungered for a taste of his ability and knowledge. One of the early protégés was a man named Bill Horn.

Continental King and Bill Horn *Photo by Dalco*

Promise Fulfilled

"He became one of our better – or the best – showmen we've had. His presentation of a Reining horse has done more for the industry than any other thing or any other person" -Dale Wilkinson

That Bill Horn was one of the most accomplished trainer/exhibitors in the history of the NRHA is a given. After all, the man who is known far and wide as "BH" won virtually every accolade that the reining horse industry has to offer.

As one of Dale Wilkinson's earliest protégés, Horn began his career with pretty big shoes to fill. This he did, and then some because, not only did he meet every expectation his taciturn mentor put before him, he raised the bar to such a height that every aspiring Wilkinson apprentice that followed in his footsteps would be sorely pressed to keep suit.

Bill Horn was, in every way, the "leader of the pack".

Bill Horn was born in Pike County, Ohio, on December 19, 1938. As the story goes, he did not even sit on a horse until he was 23. Prior to this, he worked for nine years assembling machinery in a Midwestern factory.

By the early 1960's, Bill's older brother Paul was an up-and-coming Buckeye State horse trainer. One day, Bill went out to watch Paul ride and wound up on the back of a horse. He enjoyed the experience so much that he made the decision to learn more about riding and training. Within a short span of time, he had progressed enough to hang out his shingle as a horse trainer as well.

Bill's performance on Continental King in a 1965 jackpot reining at Dayton, Ohio, inspired the formation of the National Reining Horse Association within one short year.

Bill Horn aboard 1992 NRHA Open World Champion Trashadeous.   *Photo courtesy NRHA*

The first NRHA Futurity was held in 1966. Horn won the event four times with Mr. Poco Luis (1967), Eternal One (1972), Aces Command (1981) and Spirit of Five (1987).

In addition, he earned the NRHA Futurity Reserve Championship six times with Miz Liz Dodson (1968), Glenda Echols (1971), Continental Charo (1972), Enterprise Velvet (1983), Trashadeous (1990) and Mifillena (1994). Horn was also a multiple NRHA Derby and Super Stakes Champion and he won three NRHA Open World Championships with Walkaway Rene (1978), White Is (1980) and Trashadeous (1992).

Bill Horn was inducted into the NRHA Hall of Fame in 1992. Through the years, 10 horses he rode or was associated with, have joined him in the Hall of Fame. In 1995, Horn was named NRHA's first Million Dollar Rider; and his foundation stallion, Be Ache Enterprise, was named an NRHA's second Million Dollar Sire.

The Buckeye State native served on the NRHA board from 1966 through 1994, and was president of the association in 1977. In addition, he was an active member of the NCHA and AQHA. Bill Horn passed away at his home in Ocala, Florida, on December 9, 2011, at the age of 73.

Family Connections

Dale's legacy also includes the significant contributions of his children and grandchildren.

He was blessed to have a wife like Lucy, who would take care of the house, books, records, prepare meals for unknown numbers of persons at the drop of a hat and support him in his dedication to reining and cutting horses. She also gave him three precious children, Gary, Mavis and April. Dale did not want her cleaning stalls, but the children were not so exempted.

Gary Wilkinson was born May 13, 1948. Growing up with the horse training operations,

Dale Wilkinson and Bill Horn celebrating Bill's 1992 Hall of Fame moment. **Courtesy Quarter Horse Journal**

The extended Wilkinson Family (from left to right) Matt Kiminsky, Mavis Garber, Gary Wilkinson, Sarah Wilkinson-Kaminsky, Mary Wilkinson, Nathan Wilkinson, Lucy Wilkinson, April Weaver, Rick Weaver, Megan Weaver, Meghan Willis-Wilkinson (not pictured Nick amd Dakota Garber).   **Courtesy Wilkinson Family**

he did his share of stall cleaning, fence painting, hay baling, sister watching and anything else that needed to be done. As he grew, his path became one of science, not horses. Following graduation from Heidelberg College in 1970, Gary pursued a career in applied sciences. In 1975 he received a M.S. in Science from the Department of Animal Sciences from the Ohio State University, and is a 1986 Diplomat of the American Board of Toxicology. He lives in German Village, Columbus, OH, with wife Mary. They have two children, Nathan Andrew, Educator and 2000 graduate of the College of Wooster, and Sarah Louise, a 2003 Graduate of Ohio University in Social Work, who received her M.S., at the Ohio State University in 2005.

Born June 26, 1952, Mavis has been a professional horse trainer for over 30 years. She was the first woman to compete with the men in the National Reining Horse Association. As a youth one of her biggest accomplishments was winning the All-round Reserve Championship

Gary, Mary, Nathan Andrew and Sarah Louise Wilkinson.   **Courtesy Wilkinson Family**

at the All American Quarter Horse Congress (the most prestigious Quarter Horse show in the nation.) She has won several year-end award titles in OCHA (Ohio Cutting Horse Association) and has shown and placed at the NCHA Futurity, non-pro and open divisions. Starting in 1979 she won the same NRHA class five years consecutively at the All American Quarter Horse Congress. In 1992 she won the Straight Arrow Reining Futurity (limited open division) at the All American Quarter Horse Congress and was the first woman to have placed in the NRHA open futurity. She trained Miss Maggie Jack who won the NRHA Non-Pro Pre-Futurity and went on to win the NRHA Non-Pro Futurity. She has trained, shown or helped non-pros and youths to year-end awards, world finalist, futurity titles and futurity finalists in DRHA, NRHA, GRCHA, NRCHA, FRCHA, FRHA, NCHA, OCHA. She resides on Dale's farm at Waynesboro, Georgia, where she is still involved in the horse business, breeding, training, showing, instructing and selling horses. Mavis and her husband, Nick Garber, have one son, Dakota, who is slated to attend Georgia Southern University.

April was born April 8, 1961. She attended the University of Findlay and Columbus College of Art and Design. In 1987 she married Rick Weaver and also earned a NRHA World Reserve Ladies Championship. She also is the All American Quarter Horse Congress 2004 Limited Non-Pro Futurity Champion, 2011 NRHA East Central Regional Affiliate Champion in Limited Non Pro and Reserve Champion in Intermediate Non Pro and Non Pro. Rick is involved at all levels of the reining discipline. His history with NRHA as a competitor goes back to 1977.

April, Megan and Rick Weaver. **Courtesy Wilkinson Family**

April Wilkinson and Okie Seventy Six at NRHA 1982 Maturity in Raleigh, NC.
Photo by Doug Laraby

Dale is Inducted into the NRHA Hall of Fame in 1986. *Courtesy* **Quarter Horse Journal**

Dale is inducted in to the Quarter Horse Congress Hall of Fame with David McDonald presenting the award. *Courtesy* **Quarter Horse Journal**

He was the 1982 NRHA Open Futurity Champion, '82 NRHA Derby Reserve Champion, 3-time World Championship title holder, past chairman of NRHA judges committee, as well as past president of the NRHA. At the 2009 Rolex FEI World Cup Finals, he rode Dun Its Manhattan to clinch the honors for his squad to take the International Reining Celebrity Challenge. He holds judging privileges with AQHA, NRHA, and FEI associations. He is a 2013 inductee to the NRHA Hall of Fame. He has operated Rick Weaver Reining Horses for the past 31 years. Although Rick never worked for Dale, he "worked for his daughter's hand in marriage", as Lucy Wilkinson said.

Together, April and Rick have a daughter, Megan, who is presently enrolled at

California University of Pennsylvania, majoring in Gerontology and Nursing. Some of her accomplishments include: 2002 and 2003 All American Quarter Horse Congress NRHA 13 and Under Reining Champion, 2002 NRHA Futurity Show Champion 13 and under, two-time 13 and under Saddlesmith Series Award winner, 2003 recipient of the Clayton Woosley Memorial Hi-Scoring Youth Perpetual Trophy, 2009 Fairview High School Most Valuable Senior Athlete in girls' volleyball, basketball and softball.

Superior Education

Perhaps the most significant legacy left by Dale Wilkinson is the knowledge obtained by thousands of students at the University of Findlay. Their equestrian studies major has grown into one of the premier horse-training educational programs in the United States, attracting students from all over the country and beyond. "There is not another program in the country of this size and with the caliber of instructors we have," said Steve Brown, director of the western riding program, who has been an instructor for 22 years and was a student of the program during his early years. "All our instructors are professionals in the fields and very active in the horse industry. They are judges all over the country and world. We attract serious students." According to Brown, only about 15 percent of students solely want to do training and about 95 percent have a dual major, which the university highly encourages.

Most Findlay graduates get jobs, with many ending up on the business side of the industry. "People are starting to call us all the time," said Sandra McCarthy, Director of the English Riding Program. "We have more jobs than we have kids. If you can't find a job with our degree, it's because you're not looking or you don't want to. You may not make a million dollars, but can most certainly make a living." She added that many other universities tailor their equestrian programs after Findlay's.

What a legacy from a self-taught, naturally talented Ohio farmboy.

Riders and Horses

It would be impossible to even think of trying to list all of the individuals impacted by Dale Wilkinson during his life with horses, but here is a listing of NRHA Hall of Fame Inductees with a Wilkinson Connection:

1. R. D. Baker
2. Stretch Bradley
3. Michie Glenn
4. Continental King
5. Mr Gun Smoke
6. Hollywood Smoke
7. Bill Horn
8. Jim Willoughby
9. Dick Pieper
10. Clark Bradley
11. Trashadeous
12. Dr. Tim Bartlett
13. Gunner
14. Mike Flarida
15. Rick Weaver

NCHA Hall of Fame (with Ike Hamilton)
Courtesy Quarter Horse Journal

Probably most significant connection to Dale Wilkinson would be his legacy to the horses, a legacy of loose reins, calm mouths, and fluid, soft rides with flowing maneuvers.

Wisdom

Wisdom shows itself in many ways. The following testimonial by Dale's neighbor and friend, Jerry Salter, says a great deal about Dale's broad wisdom:

"According to Webster, a legend is an admirable person for whom stories are told. ... I cannot recall the exact day I met Mr. Dale. I had heard of him and his huge horse barn, before I actually met him. Then he became a customer at our building supply store. He always had that little smirk of laughter. He had some unique projects over the years, most were rigging some type of apparatus for training or convincing a horse to do something his way. He wore old blue jeans and a white tee shirt. Not an uncommon dress for rural farming communities, until you got to the boots and spurs. They would draw a little attention. Through the years, I realize this was the uniform of a man I would come to know and respect.

"Not too many years after Mr. Dale and Mrs. Lucy moved down here, we purchased land that joins their farm. At this time, I learned he was not only an accomplished horseman, but also a civil servant. Mr. Dale served as the self-appointed Mayor of our little area on Porter Carswell Road for over 20 years. All new construction, new purchases, hay making, or fencing had to be approved by him.

"Don't try to sneak something in – that golf cart would sneak right up on you. If he didn't make it over on the weekend, he would slip over during the week and check things out when everyone else was at work and then come by the store to discuss it. The first comment would usually be, 'That looks like more work to me'.

"I will truly miss his Sunday morning visits; he always had words of wisdom. One Sunday morning, I was brushing my horse getting ready

Dale at 1999 USET Finals

Courtesy **Quarter Horse Journal**

for a ride; he wanted to know what I was doing. I said, 'I'm brushing my horse'. He said 'Um, I'm still using the same brush I started with'. It was his way of saying 'You're wasting your time grooming; you should be riding!'

"There were times when I would have the privilege to ride in the pen with Mr. Dale. He would give me a few pointers on cutting. I would just nod my head as if I understood exactly what he was saying and accept the criticism when done. He would always want me to move the horse's backend around to align with the front shoulder, or maybe it was align the right side with the left. I don't know, all I wanted to do was stay in the saddle and quit being yelled at!

"Had I not had an interest in horses, cutting horses in particular, and bought the adjoining acreage, I may have never known the accomplishments of this great man. He would never 'toot his own horn', nor capitalize on his accomplishments. He would freely give his advice, although sometimes not as straight forth as you would like. Sometimes you had to sift through the information, but there would always be something of value. He was a giver and not a taker of his skills.

"His technique to training and breeding, according to him, was simple. I got first-hand experience for this while trail riding one day. I rode up to the farm on a mare I had purchased from Mr. Dale. He said, 'That mare looks like she is in heat. I always thought she was a pretty decent mare; I think we ought to breed her.' I said, 'Okay, what's the deal?' He said, 'I get the first one; you get the next one.' So, I got off the mare, took my saddle off her, led her to the round pen where the stud was, bred her, put my saddle back on and rode home. Simple as that. Eleven months later, Dale had a pretty little colt. I had to wait another year for mine.

"Mr. Dale truly loved sports. We had a satellite dish installed at our house shortly after we moved in. Back then, the dish was the size of a small country. He rode over on his golf cart one day and said, 'I bet you can watch just about anything on TV with that thing.' I said, 'yes, sir'. He said, 'I bet you could even get the boxing match'. I said, 'Yes sir, I'm sure we can.' We watched the boxing match that weekend.

"His love for sports was passed down to his children and grandchildren. In his shy way he would tell us about his grandchildren and their success at a sport. His smiling blue eyes would twinkle with pride. His family was a great part of his life. He had a beautiful admiration for Mrs. Lucy. She was, and still is, a most devoted fan. They were truly blessed with over 60 years together.

"Mr. Dale was the toughest, strongest willed man I've ever met. After open heart surgery, hernia surgery, and while taking dialysis three times a week, he continued to ride horses and, in his words, 'try to figure out how to train one better.' But that was just his sense of humor; we know the legend had already perfected it..."

Dale Wilkinson revolutionized the reining horse industry with a few profound tips:

"You can't train a horse in a stall.
"You can't train them until you can ride them.
"I don't ride around and warm up. I don't want to mess up my train of thought!
"Every foot has to be controlled.
"His brain is the smallest part of him, but the most important.
"You ask him until he does it.
"It's not just about competing ... fall in love with the process.
"It's about a relationship with the animal
"A reiner can't stop if he's not running.
"I enjoy reining, cutting and aggravating people.
"I don't work on my Mercedes with a sledgehammer.
"Riding has been a big part of my life. It's been a good life. It's been hard, but it's been good."
— Dale Wilkinson

As his son-in-law, Rick Weaver, said at the Findlay Memorial for Dale, "he was the best listener I have ever met. He made us better people, not just better horsemen.".

Dale Wilkinson's saddle and hat are showcased in a final tribute to the "father of reining". **Courtesy Quarter Horse Journal**

Epilogue

"You Can Let Go"

The slender 84-year-old patient lay fitfully in the hospital bed – recovering from surgery to repair a recently broken hip. The man's weathered face and hands spoke to a lifetime spent outdoors, and a pair of bowed legs indicated much of that time had been spent on the back of a horse.

The man's wife and a local pastor sat by his bedside.

The man seemed ill-at-ease. He tossed and turned and tried to speak, but the words would just not come out right.

At one point, his wife asked him, "What is wrong? You seem agitated; as if there are things weighing heavily on your mind – things that you need to be doing.

"It's all right; you've enjoyed a long and full life doing what you loved. You were always meant to train horses and mentor young people who wished to follow in your footsteps.

"But God doesn't have any more horses for you to train, Dale, so you can let go."

And let go was exactly what Dale Wilkinson did – as he quietly passed from this world and into the next.

Dale Wilkinson

Photo Index

B

Beckett, Dr. Richard, 6, 88
Benny Binion's Gelding, 29
Boucher, James, 33
Bradley, Clark, 57, 58, 66, 91
Buck, 11, 13, 15, 23

C

Calhoun, Jim Jr., 24, 85
Caliche 34, 35
Clene Continental, 54
Continental King, 50, 51, 52, 99
Crawford, Todd, 69

D

Denhardt, Robert, 25
Dodge, Don, 31
Dude's Blaze, 58, 66
Dupri Katie, 61, 66

F

Flarida, Mike, 68

G

Garber, Dakota, 96
Garber, Mavis Wilkinson, 96, 102
Garber, Nick, 96
Graves, Sam, 26
Griffith, Sid, 60
Gun Smoke's Dream, 80, 82
Gun Smokes Wimpy, 82

H

Hamilton, Ide, 105
Hollywood Smoke, 82
Hollywood Snapper, 43, 44
Horn, Bill, 52, 69, 78, 82, 99, 100, 101, 102
Housekeeper, 30
Hub, 26
Hubbert, Pat, 84
Hutton, Charlie, 55

K

King P-234, 50
King of Four Mac, 55
King's Pistol, 24

L

Leo's Question, 71
Little Joe Doug, 59

M

Marian's Girl, 31
Marijuana Smoke, 76, 95
Miss Nancy Bailey, 33
Miss Liz Dodson, 53
Miss Smokette, 83
Miss White Trash, 79
M's Duchess, 37
Mr Gun Smoke, 68, 70, 74

O

Okie Seventy Six, 103
Old Paint, 27
One Gun, 83
Orphans Got Money, 96

P

Pana Smoke, 81
Patterson, Debbie, 82
Peppo's Dream, 95
Peppo's Money, 95
Play Dual Rey, 69
Pocorochie Bo, 56, 57
Poco Tivio, 32
Political Smoker, 84

R

Red Ants Snort, 60
Rondo's King, 46, 47, 49
Rondo Leo, 71
Royal King, 33
Royal King Bailey, 39, 40, 41, 42

S

Smokes Dude, 84
Smokin 45, 77
Smokin Pistol, 85
Smyth, Ray, 27
Snappy Dun, 45
Snipper W, 31
Sugar Bar Dell, 66

T

Trashadeous, 69, 100
Trodi Command, 67

W

War Leo, 72
War Olee, 73
Weaver, April Wilkinson, 81, 102, 103
Weaver, Megan, 102, 103
Weaver, Rick, 102, 103
Welch, Buster, 31
Wilkinson, Dale, 2, 11, 13, 14, 15, 16 17, 20, 21, 34, 35, 37, 39, 40, 41, 42, 43, 44, 45, 46, 47, 48, 51, 54, 56, 57, 59, 65, 74, 76, 80, 88, 95, 97, 101, 103, 104, 105, 106, 109
Wilkinson, Gary, 35, 42, 102
Wilkinson, Lucy Sherman, 22, 23, 102
Wilkinson, Mary, 102
Wilkinson, Nathan Andrew, 102
Wilkinson, Sarah Louise, 102
Willoughby, Jim, 61, 67

National Reining Horse Association
3000 NW 10th St, Oklahoma City, OK 73107-5302
Phone: (405) 946-7400 Fax: (405) 946-8425
www.nrha.com

National Cutting Horse Association
260 Bailey Ave., Fort Worth, TX 76107
Phone: (817) 244-6188, Fax: (817) 244-2015
www.nchacutting.com

American Quarter Horse Association
1600 Quarter Horse Drive, Amarillo, TX 79104
P.O. Box 200, Amarillo, TX 79168
Customer Service (806) 376-4811
Records Research (806) 376-7415
www.aqha.com

The American Quarter Horse Heritage Center & Museum
2601 I-40 East, Amarillo, TX 79104
(806) 376-5181

The American Quarter Horse Journal
1600 Quarter Horse Drive, Amarillo, TX 79104
P.O. Box 32470, Amarillo, TX 79120
(806) 376-4888 Fax: (806) 349-6400
E-mail: aqhajrnl@aqha.org

American Paint Horse Association
P.O. Box 961023 • Fort Worth, Texas 76161-0023
(817) 834-2742 • Fax (817) 834-3152
www.apha.com

Author's Profile

FRANK HOLMES was born November 3, 1947 and graduated high school from Kenmare, North Dakota in 1965. The itinerant life of an Army family led Frank to seek stability by reading and researching equine-related facts in magazines of the day. He had an uncanny ability to remember exactly where he read or saw a pedigree or horse photo. He was all things horses – tenaciously seeking out mentors from pioneer Appaloosa breeders. In doing so, he came to understand that what others may have considered ordinary people were really heroes to a young man whose passion drove him to learn and pen the history of a breed he loved. He submitted his first article to *Western Horseman* in 1961 when he was 13 years old and was published at the age of 14.

Frank spent the majority of his early working career as a federal civil servant, but writing was always his vocation. He began selling feature articles to horse magazines on a part-time basis in 1965. After almost 18 years as a civil servant, Frank decided to follow his dream as an author and equine historian. His first love in horses was the Appaloosa, and after submitting an article to the *Appaloosa Journal*, the editor commented that "Frank is the most knowledgeable man I've ever met concerning Appaloosas. If ever there could be called an Appaloosa addict, that person would be Frank Holmes. Like a baseball addict that can remember every batting average, every World Series home run, Frank can recite pedigrees and national champions like scripture."

During the 1970's and 1980's, Frank partnered with Carol Plybon in an Appaloosa breeding and show program at Caryvale Stables, Abilene, KS, standing two notable stallions, "Absarokee Rebel" and "Solid Sugar Bars." Frank loved the anticipation of foaling season, waiting to see the results from crossing a stallion and mare he had chosen. His broad knowledge of bloodlines, along with Carol's sound conditioning program, produced numerous Appaloosa halter winners.

Frank's interests have always been centered on the historical aspect of the western horse breeds, and his broad-based knowledge of the origins of the Quarter Horse, Paint, Appaloosa and Palomino registries established him as one of the pre-eminent historians of all time. As a former staff writer for *Western Horseman* magazine, Frank co-authored volumes 2 through 6 and was the sole author of volume 8 of the immensely popular *Quarter Horse Legends* book series. He also authored *The Hank Wiescamp Story* under the *Western Horseman* mantle. As the award-winning Features Editor of *The Paint Horse Journal*, he contributed a steady stream of top-notch personality profiles, genetic studies and historical overviews. Frank also published *Crystal's Vision*, a well-received children's book.

In early 2001, Frank launched LOFT Enterprises, LLC – his own publishing company. Since that time he devoted the lion's share of his journalistic efforts to the research and writing of historical books designed to capture the West's rich history and pass it on in a way that both enlightens and entertains. Among the books authored under LOFT's banner are *Wire to Wire, the Walter Merrick Story*; *More Than Color 1*; *More Than Color 2*; *Spotted Pride*; and *King P-234*.

Frank's life was more than horses – at its core, it was family and sharing his love for Jesus Christ. He worked as an Awana leader and mentored many of the youth in his church family. He loved to laugh – he laughed often and well.

While working on this latest project, Reinmaker, Frank lost his 20 year battle with cancer and passed away on January 12, 2013, surrounded by his wife and church family. He is survived by his wife, Loyce Robertson Holmes, sons Eric, Craig, Morgan Gandy and 10 beautiful grandchildren as well as three sisters, two brothers and countless friends and fans.